History Summarized
VIETNAM WAR

WORLD BOOK

www.worldbook.com

World Book, Inc.
180 North LaSalle Street
Suite 900
Chicago, Illinois 60601
USA

Copyright © 2018 (print and e-book) World Book, Inc.
All rights reserved.

This volume may not be reproduced in whole or in part in any form without prior written permission from the publisher.

WORLD BOOK and the GLOBE DEVICE are registered trademarks or trademarks of World Book, Inc.

For information about other "History Summarized" titles, as well as other World Book print and digital publications, please go to www.worldbook.com

For information about other World Book publications, call 1-800-WORLDBK (967-5325).

For information about sales to schools and libraries, call 1-800-975-3250 (United States) or 1-800-837-5365 (Canada).

Library of Congress Cataloging-in-Publication Data for this volume has been applied for.

History Summarized
ISBN: 978-0-7166-3800-1 (set, hc.)

Vietnam War
978-0-7166-3807-0 (hc.)

Also available as:
ISBN: 978-0-7166-3817-9 (e-book)

STAFF

Writer: Tom Firme

Executive Committee

President
Jim O'Rourke

Vice President and
Editor in Chief
Paul A. Kobasa

Vice President, Finance
Donald D. Keller

Vice President, Marketing
Jean Lin

Vice President, International
Maksim Rutenberg

Vice President, Technology
Jason Dole

Director, Human Resources
Bev Ecker

Editorial

Director, New Print
Tom Evans

Manager
Jeff De La Rosa

Editor
Mellonee Carrigan

Librarian
S. Thomas Richardson

Manager, Contracts and Compliance
(Rights and Permissions)
Loranne K. Shields

Manager, Indexing Services
David Pofelski

Digital

Director, Digital Product Development
Erika Meller

Digital Product Manager
Jonathan Wills

Manufacturing/Production

Manufacturing Manager
Anne Fritzinger

Production Specialist
Curley Hunter

Proofreader
Nathalie Strassheim

Graphics and Design

Senior Art Director
Tom Evans

Coordinator, Design Development and Production
Brenda Tropinski

Senior Visual Communications Designer
Melanie Bender

Senior Designer
Isaiah Sheppard

Media Editor
Rosalia Bledsoe

Senior Cartographer
John M. Rejba

TABLE OF CONTENTS

Preface: "History Summarized" 4
Introduction: What was the Vietnam War? 5
Chapter One: Background of the war 8
Chapter Two: Early stages of the war 28
Chapter Three: The fighting intensifies 40
Chapter Four: U.S. presidents, personalities,
   and leaders of the war 76
Chapter Five: Final U.S. troop withdrawal
   and end of the war 98
Index 126
Find out more!; Acknowledgments 128

"History Summarized"

Each book in this series concisely surveys a major historical event or interrelated series of events or a major cultural, economic, political, or social movement. Especially important and interesting aspects of the subject of each book are highlighted in feature sections. Use a "History Summarized" book as an introduction to its subject in preparation for deeper study or as a review of the subject to reinforce what has been studied about the topic.

INTRODUCTION

What was the Vietnam War?

The Vietnam War was the longest war in which the United States fought. It began in 1957 and ended in 1975. Vietnam, a small country in Southeast Asia, was divided at the time into the Communist Democratic Republic of Vietnam (DRV), commonly called North Vietnam, and the non-Communist Republic of Vietnam (RVN), commonly called South Vietnam. North Vietnamese and Communist-trained South Vietnamese rebels sought to overthrow the government of South Vietnam and eventually reunite the country. The United States and the South Vietnamese army tried to stop them but failed.

The Vietnam War was the second phase of fighting in Vietnam. During the first phase, which began in 1946, the Vietnamese fought France for control of Vietnam. At that time, Vietnam was part of the French colonial empire in Indochina. The United States sent France military equipment, but the Vietnamese defeated the French in 1954. Vietnam was then split into North and South Vietnam. (Indochina is the eastern half of a long and curving peninsula that extends into the South China Sea from the mainland of Southeast Asia. Indochina today consists of the three nations of Cambodia, Laos [*LAH ohs*], and Vietnam.)

United States aid to France and later to non-Communist South Vietnam was based on a Cold War policy of President Harry S. Truman (1884-1972). The Cold War was an intense rivalry between Communist and non-Communist nations. It extended from 1945 through 1991. Truman had declared that the United States must help any nation challenged by Communism. The Truman Doctrine was at first directed at Europe and the Middle East. But it was also adopted by the next three presidents, Dwight D. Eisenhower, John F. Kennedy, and Lyndon B. Johnson, and applied to Indochina. They feared that if one Southeast Asian nation joined the Communist camp, the others would also "fall," one after the other, like what Eisenhower called "a row of dominoes."

The Vietnamese Communists and their allies called the Vietnam War a war of national liberation. They saw the Vietnam War as an extension of the struggle with France and another attempt by a foreign power to rule Vietnam. North Vietnam wanted to end U.S. support of South Vietnam and reunite the north and south into a single nation. China and the Soviet Union, at that time the two largest Communist nations, gave the Vietnamese Communists war materials but not troops.

The Vietnam War had several stages. From 1957 to 1963, North Vietnam aided rebels opposed to the government of South Vietnam, which fought the rebels with U.S. aid and advisory personnel. From 1964 to 1969, North Vietnam and the United States did much of the fighting. Australia, New Zealand, the Philippines, South Korea, and Thailand also helped South Vietnam. By April 1969, the number of U.S. forces in South Vietnam had reached its peak of more than 543,000 troops. That July, the United States slowly began to withdraw its forces from the region.

In January 1973, a cease-fire was arranged. The last American ground troops left Vietnam two months later. The fighting began again soon afterward, but U.S. troops did not return to Vietnam. South Vietnam surrendered on April 30, 1975, as North Vietnamese troops entered its capital, Saigon (*SY gawn*) (now Ho Chi Minh [*hoh chee mihn*] City).

The Vietnam War was enormously destructive. Military deaths reached about 1.3 million, and the war left much of Vietnam in ruins.

Just before the war ended, North Vietnam helped rebels overthrow the U.S.-backed government in nearby Cambodia. After the war, North Vietnam united Vietnam and helped set up a new government in nearby

Demonstrations against U.S. involvement in the Vietnam War took place throughout the United States. U.S. military police (above) hold back protesters during a sit-in at the Pentagon in October 1967.

Laos. The U.S. role in the war became one of the most debated issues in the nation's history. Many Americans felt U.S. involvement was necessary and noble. But many others called it cruel, unnecessary, and wrong. Today, many Americans still disagree on the goals, conduct, and lessons of U.S. participation in the Vietnam War.

In March 1954, Communist-led Vietminh rebels launched a massive attack on French positions at the besieged Dien Bien Phu fortress (shown here), in what is now northwestern Vietnam, during the Indochina War. The Vietminh conquest of the French garrison during the Battle of Dien Bien Phu forced France to give up its colonies in Indochina.

CHAPTER ONE

Background of the war

In the late 1800's, France gained control of Indochina—that is, the countries of Vietnam, Laos, and Cambodia. Japan occupied Indochina during most of World War II (1939-1945). After Japan's defeat in 1945, Ho Chi Minh (1890-1969), a Vietnamese nationalist and Communist, and his Vietminh (*VEE eht MIHN*) (Revolutionary League for the Independence of Vietnam, in English), declared Vietnam to be independent. But France was determined to reclaim its former colonial possessions in Indochina. In 1946, war broke out between France and the Vietminh. The United States provided the French with equipment and weapons, as well as a small number of advisers, mechanics, and aircrew. Communist China and the Soviet Union supported the Vietminh.

In late November 1946, a French-Vietminh dispute led to a French naval bombardment of the northern city of Haiphong (*hy fawng*). Fighting then erupted between Vietminh and French troops in the city of Hanoi (*hah NOY*) on December 19—which is considered the starting date of the war. French and Vietminh soldiers then also clashed in Hue (*hway*), Nam Dinh, and other cities. Early in 1947, the Vietminh pulled back into the rugged Viet Bac region near the Chinese border. Fighting continued there and in other places through 1948.

In 1949, Communist forces won the civil war in China, and supplies and support flooded across the border to help the Vietminh. In response, the United States began directly aiding the French in Vietnam. That same year, the French created the Associated States of Indochina,

Ho Chi Minh

Ho Chi Minh, a Vietnamese Communist leader, served as president of North Vietnam from 1954 until his death in 1969. Ho helped Vietnam gain independence from France, which had ruled the country since the 1800's.

Ho was born on May 19, 1890, in central Vietnam. He used many names during his life, including *Nguyen Ai Quoc* (*noo yehn y kwawk*) (Nguyen the Patriot). In the early 1900's, Ho traveled and worked in Europe. He joined the French Communist Party at its founding in 1920.

At the end of World War II in 1945, Ho became head of a Vietnamese government that declared independence from France. In 1946, fighting broke out between the French and Ho's troops, known as the Vietminh. After the Vietminh defeated the French in 1954, an international conference divided Vietnam into two parts. Ho became president of North Vietnam.

In the 1950's and 1960's, Ho's Communist government sent troops to aid rebels in South Vietnam who were trying to overthrow the anti-Communist government there. Ho died on Sept. 3, 1969. His followers continued to aid the rebels after his death and, in 1975, the Communist forces won control of South Vietnam.

North Vietnamese President Ho Chi Minh (above, pointing) visited the crew of an antiaircraft unit in his Communist nation in 1967. Ho helped Vietnam gain independence from France.

which included Cambodia, Laos, and Vietnam, within the French Union. The Associated States were backed by the Americans and opposed to the DRV (North Vietnam). Former Vietnamese emperor Bao Dai (*bow DY*) headed the government of the Associated State of Vietnam.

The Vietminh—who greatly outnumbered the French—launched major attacks in 1950. An offensive in southern Vietnam failed badly, but the Vietminh took Lao Cai (*low KY*) and the French stronghold of Dong Khe (*dawng hay*) in the north. In 1951, the Vietminh suffered terrible *casualties* (people killed, wounded, missing, or captured) in failed attacks at Vinh Yen, near Hanoi; at Mao Khe (*mow hay*), near Haiphong; and along the Day River. By 1952, fighting had shifted into the mountainous Hoa Binh (*hwah bihn*) region southwest of Hanoi. In November, another Vietminh attack failed at Na San near the border with Laos.

In 1953, the French focused on preventing a Vietminh invasion of Laos, a French ally. To block attack routes into Laos, the French fortified the remote village of Dien Bien Phu (*dyehn byehn FOO*). Nearly all French troops, equipment, and supplies arrived by air. The Vietminh watched the build-up and began planning what would become the war's last major and decisive battle.

By early 1954, the Vietminh had concentrated large forces—including heavy artillery and antiaircraft guns—around Dien Bien Phu. They launched a massive assault on March 13. About 50,000 Vietminh soldiers began attacking the French force of more than 10,000 troops at the base. The Vietminh soon destroyed the French airfields, and their

Crouching low, paratroopers of the South Vietnamese Army's Airborne Division (above) advance on Vietminh positions during fighting in the Indochina War in early 1954.

The Vietminh concentrated large forces as well as heavy artillery and antiaircraft guns (shown above) around the French-fortified village of Dien Bien Phu during the Indochina War.

antiaircraft guns fired on planes dropping supplies and paratroopers over the Dien Bien Phu battlefield.

The war ended after the conquest of the French garrison of Dien Bien Phu by Vietminh forces in May. Losses for France and its allies in Indochina totaled over 90,000 killed and more than 75,000 wounded. Roughly 175,000 Vietminh died in the war, as did about 125,000 Vietnamese civilians. In July, the two sides signed peace agreements in Geneva, Switzerland.

The United States had provided aid to the French in Indochina since 1950. President Harry S. Truman had been convinced that such assistance was necessary in part because of the Communist takeover of China in 1949. Truman feared a Vietminh victory in Vietnam would lead to a Communist takeover of Indochina as part of a larger Communist plan to dominate Asia. This fear was so great that Truman ignored pleas by Ho for U.S. aid against French colonialism and for an alliance with the United States.

Vietnamese history through 1956

People have lived in what is now Vietnam since prehistoric times. Archaeologists have discovered remains of a Stone Age culture dating back about 500,000 years in the province of Thanh Hoa (*tang hwah*). Agriculture developed in northern Vietnam more than 7,000 years ago.

About 5,000 years ago, a kingdom called Van Lang emerged in the Black and Red river valleys under the rule of the Hung kings. One of the most important cultures of Van Lang, the Dong Son civilization, flourished in the valleys of the Red and Ma rivers from about 800 to 300 B.C. The Dong Son civilization is known for its elaborately decorated bronze drums.

In 258 B.C., a leader named An Duong founded the kingdom of Au Lac (*ow lahk*). In 207 B.C., an official of China's Qin (*chihn*) dynasty named Zhao Tuo (*jow toh)* (Trieu Da, in Vietnamese) founded the kingdom of Nam Viet. Nam Viet included Au Lac and several other kingdoms in what is now northern Vietnam. In 111 B.C., the Chinese Han dynasty conquered Nam Viet. Through the centuries, many Vietnamese resisted Chinese rule. But not until A.D. 939, as a result of a rebellion led by Ngo Quyen (*noh koo yehn*), did the Vietnamese gain independence.

Despite the centuries of Chinese occupation, many aspects of Viet-

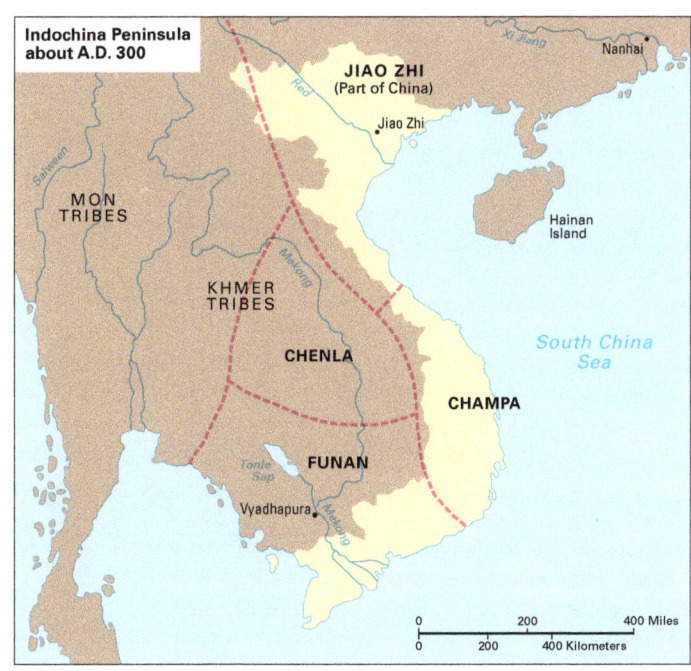

This map shows the early states of Indochina, the eastern half of a peninsula that extends from the mainland of Southeast Asia into the South China Sea. Jiao Zhi, in what is now northern Vietnam, was an independent kingdom called Nam Viet before it was conquered by China in 111 B.C. Nam Viet included Au Lac and several other kingdoms.

namese culture remained in place, but new patterns also emerged. Specifically, the rise of a mixed Chinese and Vietnamese ruling class ensured the lasting importance of Chinese writing, even though the Vietnamese continued to speak their own language. Chinese ideas of historical writing also had an enormous impact on how Vietnamese historians represented their past. Vietnamese officials sometimes adopted Chinese administrative practices. The Three Teachings—Mahayana Buddhism, Confucianism, and Taoism—are another legacy of Chinese rule.

After Ngo Quyen's death in 944, Vietnam was troubled by succession disputes and the competition of warlords. These troubles ended with the establishment of the Dinh dynasty in 968, though the dynasty lasted only 12 years. The succeeding dynasty, established in 980, lasted only until 1009. Two long-lasting dynasties, the Ly (1009-1225) and the Tran

The original Norodom Palace (shown above around 1895) served as the French colonial government headquarters in what was then Saigon (now Ho Chi Minh City), in French-ruled Vietnam. It later became the presidential palace of South Vietnamese President Ngo Dinh Diem.

(1225-1400), stabilized politics.

In 1400, Ho Quy Ly (*hoh kooy lee*) seized the Vietnamese throne, and in 1407, the Ming Chinese invaded the country and took control. In 1428, Le Loi (*leh loy*) drove out the Chinese rulers and established the Le dynasty. Under the Le rulers, the Vietnamese empire continued the process of Nam Tien (*nahm tee ehn*) (meaning Advance to the South). During the 1400's, for example, the Vietnamese conquered Champa, a rival kingdom, in what is now central Vietnam.

In 1527, the Mac dynasty overthrew the Le dynasty, and, in 1540, was formally recognized by the Ming Chinese. Le forces regained control over central Vietnam in 1545 and northern Vietnam in 1592. However,

Mac forces continued to fight against the Le for more than 35 years.

During the mid-1500's, Vietnamese politics became further fragmented as the Trinh and Nguyen (*noo yehn*) families, the two clans closest to the Le court, drifted apart. By 1600, the country was effectively divided, and the Le kept control in name only. Even though the Ming Chinese had recognized the Le dynasty as ruler of Vietnam, the Trinh lords governed the north and the Nguyen lords were in charge of the south. In the 1600's, the rivalry between these two clans occasionally erupted into armed conflict.

The Nguyen lords continued their expansion to the south until 1771. That year, three brothers from the region of Tay Son in central Vietnam began a series of successful attacks against Nguyen rule. This upheaval, known as the Tay Son Rebellion, caused the collapse of Nguyen power in the south, Trinh power in the north, and, in 1788, the end of the Le dynasty. After defending Vietnam against an invasion of Qing (*cheeng*) Chinese troops in 1789, the Tay Son dynasty tried to consolidate its rule over all of what is now Vietnam.

In 1802, Nguyen Anh (*noo yehn ang*) became the first emperor of the Nguyen dynasty. He took the reign name of Gia Long (*zah lawng*). He united the country and called it Vietnam. The Nguyen dynasty, Vietnam's last, established its capital in Hue. The dynasty formally ended in 1945.

In 1858, French warships captured the city of Da Nang. The French claimed that they were protecting Jesuit missionaries and Vietnamese who had converted to Roman Catholicism. By continuing the armed attacks and through diplomatic pressure, France succeeded in taking control of the southern part of Vietnam, known then as Cochin China, in the 1860's. In the 1880's, France took control of the northern (Tonkin) and central (Annam) parts of Vietnam. With the conquest of Cambodia in the 1860's and of Laos in the 1890's, French control of Indochina was complete.

The French were principally interested in Vietnam and the surrounding area as a base for trading with China. They also hoped to exploit the mineral wealth of Vietnam and to establish plantations for coffee, rubber, and tea. To help carry out these plans, the French built roads and railways, which linked the lowlands, midlands, and mountains. They also expanded port facilities.

Under French rule, the traditional Vietnamese ruling class withdrew from public life, and a new French-Vietnamese ruling class emerged. The romanized written version of Vietnamese known as *quoc ngu* (*kwok noo oo*) also became more prominent in private and public affairs.

Through the years, Vietnamese resistance to French rule grew. Various nationalist associations and societies emerged, as did several political parties. These parties included the Vietnamese Nationalist Party, Indochinese Communist Party, and the New Vietnamese Revolutionary Party.

In August 1940, during World War II, France's wartime Vichy (*VIHSH ee* or *vee SHEE*) government granted Japan permission to use northern Vietnam for military operations. When Japanese troops advanced into other Southeast Asian colonies of European powers, they took control of the colonial governments. In Vietnam, the Japanese at first allowed French officials to continue to carry out their administrative duties. However, in March 1945, the Japanese ousted the French officials.

Initially, most Vietnamese had welcomed the Japanese, expecting that they would free Vietnam from French rule. When Japan became a threat to their independence, many Vietnamese reconsidered their plans to join with the Japanese to fight the French. One result of such reconsideration was the creation of an organization called the Vietminh in 1941.

This map shows French Indochina, which included Cambodia and Laos in the west, and Vietnam in the east. France divided Vietnam into Tonkin, Annam, and Cochin China. France gained control of Indochina in the 1800's and held it until the 1950's.

Established by Ho Chi Minh and other Indochinese Communist Party leaders, the Vietminh was designed to encourage national unity and independence.

Japan agreed to surrender on Aug. 14, 1945. Within days, anticolonial activists in Vietnam staged the August Revolution. On September 2, Ho recited Vietnam's declaration of independence, in which he quoted

Background of the war 19

directly from the American Declaration of Independence. Ho and other revolutionary leaders expected that the United States would support the new postcolonial state—the Democratic Republic of Vietnam (DRV). They believed that they would receive such support for several reasons. For instance, the United States had gained its own independence through a revolution. The United States had also criticized European colonialism for most of the 1900's. In addition, the Vietminh had cooperated with U.S. diplomatic and military personnel during World War II. However, the DRV never received U.S. support, mainly because of U.S. opposition to Communism.

On May 7, 1954, French forces surrendered when the Vietminh overwhelmed their garrison at Dien Bien Phu after a 56-day siege. Under the guard of Vietminh soldiers, a column of captured French soldiers (below) march from the battlefield to a prisoner-of-war camp.

After World War II, France tried to reclaim its former colonies in Southeast Asia. In 1946, war broke out between France and the Vietminh. Throughout the war, the French controlled cities in north and south Vietnam. The revolutionaries, based in the mountains of the north and northwest, controlled most of the countryside. Many southern Vietnamese rejected the idea of a Communist-dominated government and sided with the French. By mid-1949, the French had formed the Associated State of Vietnam to oppose the Vietminh. Bao Dai, the last of the Nguyen emperors, headed the government of the Associated State. The fighting in Vietnam ended in May 1954, when the Vietminh over-

During the final stages of the First Indochina War, negotiators representing nine countries assembled in Geneva, Switzerland (shown at right), and produced a series of agreements known as the Geneva Accords. One of the agreements called for temporarily dividing Vietnam into northern and southern zones at the 17th parallel.

whelmed the French garrison at Dien Bien Phu.

Fearing the growth of Communism, the United States began in 1948 to channel aid to the countries of Western Europe to help them rebuild after the devastation of World War II. The assistance provided by the Marshall Plan made it possible for France to rebuild and to continue fighting the war in Vietnam. Further expressing its support for the French attempt to reconquer Vietnam, the United States formally recognized the Associated State of Vietnam in 1950.

During the final stages of the First Indochina War, negotiators repre-

senting nine countries—Cambodia, China, France, Laos, the United Kingdom, the United States, the Soviet Union, the Democratic Republic of Vietnam, and the Associated State of Vietnam—assembled in Geneva, Switzerland. In July 1954, the representatives produced a series of agreements known as the Geneva Accords. One of these agreements set out that Vietnam would be temporarily divided into northern and southern zones at the 17th parallel. Another agreement called for an election in 1956 to unify the country. Fearing that the Vietnamese Communist leader Ho Chi Minh would win such an election, however,

Vo Nguyen Giap

Vo Nguyen Giap (*vo noo yehn zap*) (1911-2013) was a Vietnamese Communist leader. He was the commander and chief military strategist of what became known as the People's Army of Vietnam (PAVN) from 1944 to 1973. His forces used such tactics as guerrilla warfare to defeat the armies of larger, more powerful countries.

In 1937, after studying Marxism and military history, Giap became a member of the Indochinese Communist Party (ICP). In 1941, Giap helped Ho Chi Minh, a Vietnamese nationalist and leader of the ICP, create the Vietminh. The Vietminh was a Communist-influenced political group that organized resistance to French colonial rule and, later, Japanese occupation. During World War II (1939-1945), Japan took control of what is now Vietnam from the French. In December 1944, Giap founded a small military unit that eventually grew to become the PAVN.

After Japan's defeat in World War II, Vietnam declared its independence on Sept. 2, 1945. However, France tried that year to reclaim its former colony, and the First Indochina War began in 1946. In May 1954, Giap and the PAVN defeated the better trained and equipped French army at the Battle of Dien Bien Phu, ending the war. A major factor in France's overall defeat was Giap's use of a strategy called *people's war,* which emphasized the total commitment of people and resources and used a combination of guerrilla and conventional warfare.

After the war, agreements called the Geneva Accords divided Vietnam into the Communist Democratic Republic of Vietnam (DRV), commonly called North Vietnam, and the non-Communist

Vietminh General Vo Nguyen Giap (right, wearing boots) surveyed the battlefield after his forces defeated the French at Dien Bien Phu.

Republic of Vietnam (RVN), commonly called South Vietnam.

In the late 1950's, tensions began escalating between the DRV and RVN. During the Vietnam War, also called the Second Indochina War, Giap led the PAVN in a drive to overthrow South Vietnam and eventually reunite Vietnam. Giap's forces continued to use people's war. RVN and United States forces tried to stop them but failed. In 1973, Giap resigned as commander of the PAVN but remained active in the government. DRV forces eventually took over South Vietnam, and the war ended on April 30, 1975.

Giap was born in An Xa (*ahn sah*), a small village in north-central Vietnam, on Aug. 25, 1911. In 1937, he earned a bachelor's degree in law and political economics from the University of Hanoi. After the Vietnam War ended, Giap held major political posts until 1982 and retired from politics in the early 1990's. He died on Oct. 4, 2013, at the age of 102.

Ho Chi Minh (left), president of the Democratic Republic of Vietnam (known as North Vietnam), attended a banquet in Beijing with Chinese Prime Minister Zhou Enlai (also spelled Chou En-lai) during Ho's visit to the Chinese capital on June 26, 1955.

the southern Vietnamese, with U.S. support, refused to participate. The election was never held.

After 1954, Ho Chi Minh strengthened the rule of his Communist government in the Democratic Republic of Vietnam, which became known as North Vietnam. Ho appointed Pham Van Dong (*fahm vahn dong*) (1906-2000) as premier in 1955. Dong, who had learned Communist revolutionary methods from Ho, long served as his country's leading spokesman on foreign affairs. Dong led the delegation of the Democratic Republic of Vietnam at the 1954 Geneva conference.

Ho Chi Minh suppressed non-Communist political parties. He also enacted land reforms and established legal equality between men and women. Ho hoped the elections of 1956 would provide him with the means to peacefully reunify the country under his revolutionary government, but the elections never occurred.

The United States moved to make the division of Vietnam permanent by helping leaders in the southern half form a non-Communist Republic of Vietnam, which became known as South Vietnam. Ngo Dinh Diem (*uhng oh dihn zih ehm*) (1901-1963), who had once refused a place in Ho Chi Minh's Communist government and vigorously opposed any Communist influence in his country, became president of South Vietnam in 1955.

With the approval of the United States, Diem refused to go along with the proposed nationwide elections scheduled for the following year. He argued that the Communists would not permit fair elections in North Vietnam. However, most experts believe that Ho Chi Minh was so popular that he would have won the elections under any circumstances. United States President Dwight D. Eisenhower (1890-1969) provided economic aid and sent several hundred U.S. civilian and military advisers to assist Diem.

Tension increased between Communists in North Vietnam and non-Communists in South Vietnam. The United States's desire to contain Communism in the region inspired its support of Diem's refusal to participate in nationwide elections, which had been called for during the 1954 Geneva Accords. This refusal became a calculated risk, the foundation of which became more unstable as Diem's government came under fire within five years after he took office. As Diem's government became threatened, the United States military presence grew and fighting developed.

In March 1963, more than 840 South Vietnamese paratroopers jumped from U.S. Air Force transport planes for an assault on the Viet Cong in Tay Ninh Province in South Vietnam. South Vietnamese President Ngo Dinh Diem described anyone who resisted his rule as Viet Cong, whether they were Communist or not.

CHAPTER TWO

Early stages of the war

Ngo Dinh Diem suppressed all rival political groups in South Vietnam in his effort to strengthen his government. But his regime never achieved widespread popularity, especially in rural areas, where his administration did little to ease the hard life of the peasants. Diem became increasingly unpopular in 1956, when he ended local elections and appointed his own officials down to the village level, where self-government was an ancient and honored tradition. From 1957 to 1959, he sought to eliminate members of the Vietminh who had joined other South Vietnamese in rebelling against his rule. Diem called these rebels the Viet Cong, meaning *Vietnamese Communists*. These rebels were largely trained by the Communists, but many were not Communist Party members.

Although North Vietnam had hoped to achieve its goals without a military conflict against the United States or the South Vietnamese government, it supported the revolt against Diem from its early stages. In 1959, as U.S. advisers rushed aid to South Vietnam by sea, North Vietnam developed a supply route to South Vietnam through Laos and Cambodia. This system of roads and trails became known as the Ho Chi Minh Trail. Also in 1959, two U.S. military advisers were killed during a battle. They were the first American casualties of the war.

By 1960, discontent with the Diem government was widespread, and the Viet Cong had about 10,000 troops. In 1961, they threatened to overthrow Diem's unpopular government. In response, U.S. President

The Viet Cong

The Viet Cong were South Vietnamese guerrillas who fought South Vietnamese and United States military forces during the Vietnam War. (*Guerrillas* are fighters who harass an enemy by sudden raids, ambushes, destruction of supply routes, and similar activities.) The Communist government of North Vietnam supported the Viet Cong. The guerrillas sought to overthrow South Vietnam's government and unite North and South Vietnam.

The Viet Cong began as a Vietnamese nationalist group called the Vietminh (Revolutionary League for the Independence of Vietnam). In 1946, the Vietminh began a long war against the French forces in Vietnam, which was then a colony of French Indochina. The Communist leader Ho Chi Minh headed the Vietminh.

In 1957, South Vietnamese President Ngo Dinh Diem began to crack down on Communists and other political groups in his country. Diem described anyone who resisted his rule as Viet Cong, whether they were Communists or not. The term *cong* is scornful slang for *Communists*. Diem's actions increased opposition to his rule and drove many non-Communists into an alliance with the Communists.

In 1960, various anti-Diem groups formed the National Liberation Front (NLF). The NLF's military wing, called the People's Liberation Armed Forces, was labeled the Viet Cong by its opponents. With North Vietnamese backing, the Viet Cong waged a successful guerrilla war against Diem's army. The United States,

Viet Cong guerrillas cross a river in boats in 1966 to fight against South Vietnam's government during the Vietnam War.

which wanted to stop the spread of Communism, responded by sending thousands of troops to South Vietnam in 1965. North Vietnam, in turn, sent thousands of its troops. In the late 1960's, Viet Cong casualties began to mount, and North Vietnam switched its focus to conventional warfare. As a result, the Viet Cong played a lesser role in the rest of the war.

Viet Cong soldiers (right) advance under covering fire from a heavy machine gun in an attack during the Vietnam War. The Viet Cong were South Vietnamese guerrillas who fought against South Vietnamese and United States forces. The group sought to overthrow the government of South Vietnamese President Ngo Dinh Diem, who ordered a crackdown on Communists and other political groups in his country. The Viet Cong fought to unite North and South Vietnam.

Early stages of the war 33

Tim O'Brien

American author Tim O'Brien (1946-   ) gained recognition for his books based on the United States involvement in the Vietnam War from 1964 to 1973. O'Brien served in the U.S. Army infantry in Vietnam in 1969 and 1970. In his partly autobiographical novels and short stories, O'Brien explores his experiences before, during, and after the war. He portrays incidents from a variety of points of view, mixing fact and fiction.

O'Brien's best-known novels are *Going After Cacciato* (1978) and *The Things They Carried* (1990). *Going After Cacciato* resembles a collection of related short stories. Cacciato is an American soldier who tries to walk away from the Vietnam War, but is found dead near the border between Vietnam and Laos. The novel is a mixture of realistic accounts of the fighting with dreamlike fantasies flowing through the mind of Paul Berlin. Berlin, an American soldier, is a member of the search party assigned to find Cacciato. *The Things They Carried* is a memoir that mixes fiction and nonfiction about incidents in the war. A character named Tim O'Brien is the book's narrator.

O'Brien's first book was a work of nonfiction, *If I Die in a Combat Zone, Box Me Up and Ship Me Home* (1973). The book is an account

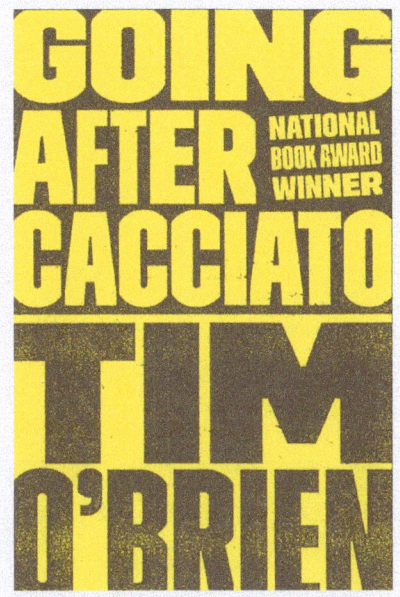 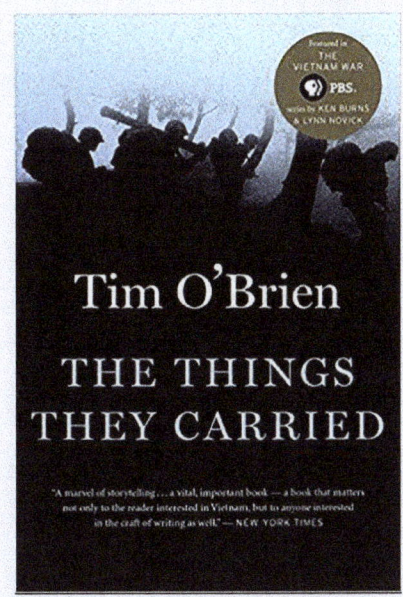

American author Tim O'Brien mixes fact and fiction in his best-selling Vietnam War-era novels *Going After Cacciato* (1978) and *The Things They Carried* (1990).

of O'Brien's tour of duty in Vietnam. It became noted for its vivid portrayal of the futility and despair he saw in war.

William Timothy O'Brien, Jr., was born on Oct. 1, 1946, in Austin, Minnesota. At the age of 7, he moved with his family to the rural town of Worthington. The small towns of Minnesota form the background for some of his fiction. O'Brien received a B.A. degree in political science from Macalaster College in 1968. After leaving the Army, he attended Harvard University, where he studied government. O'Brien then worked as a national affairs reporter for *The Washington Post* in 1973 and 1974 before devoting himself to writing full-time.

John F. Kennedy (1917-1963) greatly expanded economic and military aid to South Vietnam. From 1961 to 1963, he increased the number of U.S. military advisers in Vietnam from about 900 to more than 16,000 when the Communists threatened South Vietnam and Thailand. Kennedy also sent advisers to Laos. In addition, he sent former Republican senator and vice presidential candidate Henry Cabot Lodge, Jr., to South Vietnam as ambassador in 1963.

United States military forces established bases in Da Nang (*dah nahng*), also called Tourane (*too RAHN*), a large city in South Vietnam near the South China Sea that was an important trading center. The city would become a favorite target of the North Vietnamese forces.

In May 1963, widespread unrest broke out among Buddhists in South Vietnam's major cities. The Buddhists, who formed a majority of the country's population, complained that the government restricted their religious practices. Buddhist leaders accused Diem, a Roman Catholic, of religious discrimination. They claimed that he favored Catholics with lands and offices at the expense of local Buddhists. The government responded to the Buddhist protests with mass arrests, and Diem's brother Ngo Dinh Nhu (*noh dihn nyoo*) ordered raids against Buddhist temples. Several Buddhist monks set themselves on fire as a form of protest.

The Buddhist protests aroused great concern in the United States. The U.S. government severely criticized Diem's government for its repressive policies against the Buddhists. Kennedy urged Diem to improve his dealings with the Buddhists, but Diem ignored the advice. Kennedy then supported a group of South Vietnamese generals who opposed Diem's policies. On Nov. 1, 1963, the generals overthrew the Diem government. Diem and Nhu were murdered.

The fall of the Diem government set off a period of political disorder in South Vietnam. New governments rapidly succeeded one another. During

In May 1963, widespread unrest broke out among Buddhists in South Vietnam's major cities over religious discrimination. The government responded to the protests with mass arrests of monks and nuns (shown above) and raids on Buddhist temples.

this period, North Vietnam stepped up its supply of war materials and began to send units of its own army into the south. By late 1964, the Viet Cong controlled up to 75 percent of South Vietnam's population.

In 1964, United States President Lyndon B. Johnson approved secret South Vietnamese naval raids against North Vietnam. Just after one of these raids, on Aug. 2, 1964, North Vietnamese torpedo boats attacked

the U.S. destroyer *Maddox,* which was monitoring the impact of the raid off the coast of North Vietnam in the Gulf of Tonkin. Johnson warned the North Vietnamese that another such attack would bring "grave consequences." On August 4, he announced that North Vietnamese boats had again launched an attack in the gulf, this time against the *Maddox* and another U.S. destroyer, the *C. Turner Joy.*

Some Americans doubted that the August 4 attack had occurred, and it has never been confirmed. Nevertheless, Johnson ordered immediate air strikes against North Vietnam. He also asked Congress for power to take "all necessary measures to repel any armed attack against the forces of the United States and to prevent further aggression."

On August 7, Congress approved these powers in the Tonkin Gulf

*The USS **Maddox** (shown here) was attacked by North Vietnam torpedo boats following secret raids by South Vietnam's navy in international waters off the coast of North Vietnam in August 1964. The unprovoked attacks occured while the U.S. destroyer was monitoring the impact of the raids in the Gulf of Tonkin. The attacks led U.S. President Lyndon B. Johnson to order air strikes against North Vietnam.*

Resolution. The United States did not declare war on North Vietnam, but Johnson used the resolution as the legal basis for increased U.S. involvement. In March 1965, he sent a group of U.S. Marines to South Vietnam, the first American ground combat forces to enter the war.

With the Gulf of Tonkin Resolution, the United States became fully invested in major combat against Communist forces fighting in Vietnam. In preceding years, the U.S. military presence had incrementally increased. Following the resolution, the United States vastly expanded its combat forces through the late 1960's. The United States and its allies fought hard to crush North Vietnam and the Viet Cong troops, but struggled to gain an edge. Meanwhile, the American public began losing patience with the long-running war.

Early stages of the war

U.S. forces in Vietnam rose from about 60,000 in mid-1965 to a peak of over 543,000 in 1969. The United States relied mainly on the bombing of North Vietnam and "search and destroy" ground missions in South Vietnam to force the enemy to stop fighting. This image shows U.S. Army Captain Robert Bacon leading a ground patrol in the early years of the Vietnam War.

CHAPTER THREE

The fighting intensifies

The war soon became an international conflict. U.S. forces rose from about 60,000 in mid-1965 to a peak of over 543,000 in 1969. They joined about 800,000 South Vietnamese troops and a total of about 69,000 troops from Australia, New Zealand, the Philippines, South Korea, and Thailand. The North Vietnamese and the Viet Cong had over 300,000 troops, but the exact number is unknown.

Pham Van Dong (*fahm vahn dong*) (1906-2000), the premier of North Vietnam, signed agreements with China, the Soviet Union, and other Communist nations, providing financial and military aid for North Vietnam during the Vietnam War.

The two sides developed strategies to take advantage of their strengths. The United States had the finest modern weapons and a highly professional military force. Its field commanders were General William C. Westmoreland (1914-2005) from 1964 to 1968 and, afterward, generals Creighton Abrams (1914-1974) and Frederick Weyand (1916-2010). The United States did not try to conquer North Vietnam. Instead, American leaders hoped superior U.S. firepower would force the enemy to stop fighting. The United States relied mainly on the bombing of North Vietnam and "search and destroy" ground missions in South Vietnam to achieve its aim.

The United States used giant B-52 bombers as well as smaller planes for the main air strikes against the enemy. American pilots used helicopters to seek out Viet Cong troops in the jungles and mountains.

William C. Westmoreland

U.S. General William Childs Westmoreland (1914-2005) commanded United States forces in the Vietnam War from 1964 to 1968. He relied on ground operations that stressed the number of enemy dead over territory gained, a policy that became known as "search and destroy." In 1967, Westmoreland made several optimistic reports on United States progress in the war. But in early 1968, enemy attacks on the major cities of South Vietnam raised doubts about the war's outcome. Later that year, Westmoreland returned to the United States to serve as Army chief of staff. He retired in 1972.

In 1982, a CBS television documentary, "The Uncounted Enemy: A Vietnam Deception," charged that Westmoreland underestimated enemy strength in 1967 and 1968 to make it appear that U.S. forces were winning the war. Westmoreland sued CBS, claiming that its charges about the underestimated troop figures were false and had damaged his reputation. During the trial, some former high-ranking military officials supported the CBS charges. Soon afterward, Westmoreland and CBS officials reached an agreement to drop the suit. They issued statements pledging mutual respect for each other, but CBS also stood by its broadcast.

Westmoreland was born on March 26, 1914, in Spartanburg County, South Carolina. He graduated from the United States Military Academy in 1936. During World War II (1939-1945), Westmoreland commanded artillery forces in North Africa, Sicily, and northern Europe. He led a paratroop regiment and became a brigadier general during the Korean War (1950-1953). He became a lieutenant general in 1963. Westmoreland died on July 18, 2005.

U.S. General William Westmoreland (center) held a news conference at the White House on U.S. progress in the Vietnam War in 1968. He was joined by U.S. President Lyndon B. Johnson (right) and Secretary of State Dean Rusk (left).

The fighting intensifies

The United States used the giant B-52 Stratofortress for the main air strikes in the Vietnam War. A B-52 bomber is shown here dropping bombs over Vietnam in the 1960's. Pilots and aircrew nicknamed the B-52 "BUFF," which stood for Big Ugly Fat Fellow.

The fighting intensifies 45

Helicopters also carried the wounded to hospitals and brought supplies to troops in the field.

In contrast, Viet Cong and North Vietnamese leaders adopted a defensive strategy. Their more lightly armed troops relied on surprise and mobility. They tried to avoid major battles in the open, where heavy U.S. firepower could be decisive. The Viet Cong and North Vietnamese preferred guerrilla tactics, including ambushes and hand-laid bombs. Their advantages included knowledge of the terrain and large amounts of war materials from the Soviet Union and China.

From 1965 to 1967, the two sides fought to a highly destructive draw. The U.S. bombing caused tremendous damage, but it did not affect the enemy's willingness or ability to continue fighting. North Vietnam concealed its most vital resources, and the Soviet Union and China helped make up North Vietnam's losses.

American victories in ground battles in South Vietnam also failed to sharply reduce the number of enemy troops there. The U.S. Army and Marines usually won whenever they fought the enemy. But North Vietnam replaced its losses with new troops. Its forces often avoided defeat by retreating into neighboring Laos and Cambodia.

The Battle of Long Tan was an important battle of the Vietnam War. It took place on Aug. 18, 1966, in the southern part of what is now Vietnam. In the Battle of Long Tan, Australian troops defeated a much larger force of Viet Cong troops, who were reinforced by soldiers from the North Vietnamese Army. Long Tan was a village near the battlefield.

Australia's opposition to Communism and support for the United States led to its involvement in the Vietnam War. In 1962, Australia sent Army advisers to South Vietnam. The first Australian troops followed three years later. In 1966, the government increased Australia's commitment to the war and sent its first drafted soldiers.

The Battle of Long Tan began on Aug. 18, 1966. A small group of Australian soldiers defeated a large force of Communist-led South Vietnamese guerrillas called the Viet Cong at a rubber plantation near the village of Long Tan. The Viet Cong were reinforced by North Vietnamese Army soldiers. The two sides battled for about three hours in the pouring rain. Nightfall and the arrival of Australian reinforcements ended the battle.

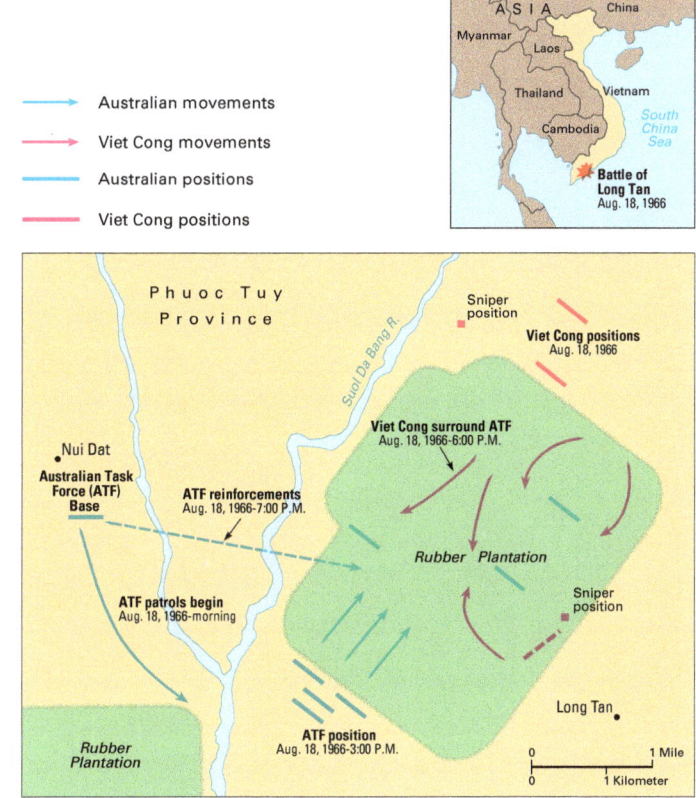

In April 1966, the Australians began to set up an operational base at Nui Dat (*noo ee daht*), about 3 miles (5 kilometers) west of Long Tan. The base was about 70 miles (110 kilometers) east of Saigon (now Ho Chi Minh City), the South Vietnamese capital. On the morning of Aug. 17, 1966, the Viet Cong fired artillery at Nui Dat. The Australians then sent out soldiers to find the Viet Cong.

On August 18, an Australian group searched for the Viet Cong at a rubber plantation near Long Tan. The group, led by Major Harry Smith, consisted of 105 Australians and 3 New Zealanders. At about 3:40 p.m., the Australians battled a small group of Viet Cong. About half an hour later, the Australians encountered the main body of Viet Cong troops.

The fighting intensifies   47

In 1969, Australian soldiers raised the Long Tan Cross (above) at the site of the Battle of Long Tan, in which a small force of Australians defeated a much larger group of Viet Cong troops. The cross is one of only two memorials permitted in Vietnam that honors a former enemy.

Experts estimate that the Viet Cong numbered more than 2,000.

In a monsoon rain, Smith's force fought the Viet Cong. American and Australian forces supported Smith's company with artillery fired from the base at Nui Dat. During the battle, two helicopters braved the rain and enemy fire to resupply Smith's troops. The Australians stopped several waves of Viet Cong attacks. Around 7:00 p.m., after about three hours of fighting, additional Australian troops reinforced Smith's company. Nightfall and the arrival of reinforcements ended the battle.

Over the course of the Battle of Long Tan, the Australians suffered 17 killed and 24 wounded. One of the wounded soldiers died from his injuries a few days later. After the battle, the Australians buried 245 Viet Cong soldiers found on the battlefield. However, captured documents indicated that hundreds more Viet Cong were killed or wounded. United States President Lyndon B. Johnson awarded Smith's company the Presidential Unit Citation for their courage.

In 1969, Australian soldiers raised the Long Tan Cross at the battle site to commemorate the battle. After the war, local villagers removed the cross. In 1989, the local government placed a replica cross at the site of the battle. In 2002, the Australian Veterans' Vietnam Reconstruction Group (AVVRG) restored the replica cross and memorial site with assistance from the Australian and Vietnamese governments. The AVVRG (now the Australia Vietnam Volunteers Resource Group) undertakes humanitarian projects in Vietnam.

The Long Tan Cross is one of only two memorials permitted in Vietnam that honors a former enemy. The other memorial, the tomb of the French soldiers, in Dien Bien Phu, commemorates the 1954 battle there, in which Vietnamese revolutionaries defeated colonial French forces.

Australia's Vietnam Veterans Day is commemorated annually on August 18, the anniversary of the Battle of Long Tan.

In 1967, Nguyen Van Thieu (*noo yehn vahn tee oh*) (1923-2001), who was a key figure in the 1963 overthrow of the Diem government, became president of South Vietnam, two years after becoming deputy prime minister and defense minister. From 1965 to 1967, he had served as chief of state and chairman of the Directory, a 10-member executive committee in the military government that ruled South Vietnam.

As the Vietnam War dragged on, it divided many Americans into so-called *hawks* and *doves*. The hawks supported the nation's fight against Communism. But they disliked Johnson's policy of slow, gradual troop increases and urged a decisive defeat of North Vietnam. The doves

Weapons of the Vietnam War

U.S. Air Force

From 1961 to 1973, the United States Air Force dropped a much greater tonnage of conventional bombs in Southeast Asia than had been dropped by both sides in World War II. Most of this bombing was conducted in the jungles of South Vietnam by B-52's and fighter aircraft against Communist rebels and their North Vietnamese allies. The simultaneous bombing of North Vietnam was done mostly by F-105 Thunderchief and F-4 Phantom fighter bombers. Before the end of the war, the Air Force had developed laser-guided bombs, which rarely missed their targets.

U.S. Navy

The U.S. Navy entered combat in South Vietnam in 1964. The Seventh Fleet launched air strikes from aircraft carriers and bombarded enemy forces and positions ashore from cruisers, destroyers, and the battleship USS *New Jersey*. The Navy's Coastal Surveillance Force, River Patrol Force, and Riverine Assault Force operated along South Vietnam's coast and on its rivers. By 1973, the Navy had turned its responsibilities in Vietnam over to South Vietnam.

U.S. Army

By 1965, the U.S. commitment to South Vietnam had grown, and large Army units went into action. The airmobile unit proved very effective in a war that required the ability to strike with surprise. The helicopter was a major weapon used by the U.S. military. Helicopters were used for attack, reconnaissance, and troop and cargo transport, as well as for ambulance service. American pilots used helicopters to seek out Viet Cong troops in the jungles and mountains and to rescue other pilots shot down in enemy territory.

The United States Air Force mainly used F-105 and F-4 fighters to carry out simultaneous bombing of North Vietnam. This F-105, shown above carrying a full bomb load, was shot down over Laos on Dec. 24, 1968, while conducting an afternoon strike mission.

During the Vietnam War, the USS *New Jersey* was the only active battleship in any of the world's navies. It is the most decorated battleship in United States naval history.

The fighting intensifies 51

The AH-1 Cobra helicopter (above), used by the U.S. military in Vietnam, was the first helicopter designed as an attack aircraft. Attack helicopters carry guns and missiles and can turn and fire almost instantly in nearly any direction.

The UH-1 Huey helicopter was used first in Vietnan and later wherever U.S. forces had been committed. During the Vietnam War, the Huey was more versatile than any other aircraft. It ferried U.S. forces into and out of combat, brought supplies, and rushed the wounded to hospitals.

The Douglas AC-47 gunship was the first such aircraft developed by the United States Air Force for service during the Vietnam War. The C-47 provided more firepower in certain situations where American ground forces called for close air support during combat.

The U.S. Air Force pressed the C-130 Hercules into action during the Vietnam War to drop off American troops and supplies or pick up the wounded in remote locations in Vietnam. The last C-130 out of Vietnam before the fall of Saigon airlifted 452 people from the besieged South Vietnamese capital in 1975.

opposed U.S. involvement and held mass protests. Many doves believed that U.S. security was not at risk. Others charged that the nation was supporting corrupt, undemocratic, and unpopular governments in South Vietnam.

However, the growing costs of the war probably did more to arouse public uneasiness in the United States than the antiwar movement did. By late 1967, increased casualties and President Johnson's request for new taxes helped produce a sharp drop in public support for the war.

Vocal opponents in the U.S. Congress included U.S. Senators Birch Bayh (1928-   ), an Indiana Democrat; John Cooper (1901-1991), a Kentucky Republican who was coauthor of the Cooper-Church amendment, which prohibited the use of U.S. ground combat forces in Cambodia without congressional approval; William Fulbright (1905-1995), a Democrat from Arkansas who was the chairman of the Senate Foreign Relations Committee from 1959 to 1974 and a spokesman for those who wanted Congress to have more control over presidential war-making powers; and Eugene McCarthy (1916-2005), a Democrat from Minnesota.

McCarthy, who served as a United States senator from 1959 to 1971, became a leading candidate for the 1968 Democratic presidential nomination. As a candidate, he consolidated the widespread opposition to the Vietnam War. He attracted much student support and won primary elections in Wisconsin and Oregon. He was narrowly defeated by President Johnson in the opening primary in New Hampshire.

McCarthy's success in the New Hampshire primary influenced U.S. Senator Robert F. Kennedy of New York to enter the Democratic race. It also helped persuade Johnson not to run for reelection. McCarthy lost in four states to Kennedy, but Kennedy was assassinated in June 1968, and Vice President Hubert H. Humphrey won the Democratic nomination.

A former member of Congress who rose as a major opponent of U.S.

Democratic Senator Eugene McCarthy of Minnesota was a vocal opponent of the Vietnam War. As a candidate for the 1968 Democratic presidential nomination, McCarthy consolidated the widespread opposition to the war and attracted much student support. Vice President Hubert H. Humphrey won the Democratic nomination.

involvement in Vietnam was Jeannette Rankin (1880-1973), a Montana Republican. She served in the House of Representatives as the first female member of Congress from 1917 to 1919 and returned for another term from 1941 to 1943. Rankin was a lifelong pacifist (opponent of violence and war) and social activist who voted against U.S. participation in World War I in 1917 and cast the only vote in Congress against entering World War II in 1941. She led the Jeannette Rankin Brigade, in which some 5,000 women Vietnam War protesters marched on Wash-

Jeanette Rankin (right), a Montana Republican, was the first woman elected to the United States Congress. She became a major opponent of U.S. involvement in Vietnam.

At the age of 87, Jeannette Rankin (center, wearing eyeglasses) led the Jeannette Rankin Brigade, in which 5,000 women protesters in boots (right) marched on Washington, D.C., in 1968 to call for an end to the Vietnam War.

ington, D.C., in January 1968. The Jeannette Rankin Brigade presented a peace petition to House Speaker John McCormack of Massachusetts.

Tet Offensive; Vietnamization

North Vietnam and the Viet Cong opened a new phase of the war on Jan. 30, 1968, when they started to attack military bases and major cities in South Vietnam. The fighting was especially fierce in Saigon, South Vietnam's capital, and in Hue. This campaign began the day before Tet, the Vietnamese New Year holiday. The Viet Cong, backed by forces from Communist North Vietnam, employed such tactics as a siege of an isolated U.S. Marine unit at Khe Sanh (*hay sahn*) in central Vietnam. This action was intended to divert attention away from the assault on the cities.

North Vietnam and the Viet Cong hoped the offensive would deal a serious blow to U.S. forces and make the South Vietnamese people lose faith in their government and rise up against South Vietnamese leaders. They also hoped that the offensive would persuade U.S. officials to enter peace negotiations with North Vietnamese leaders.

The Tet Offensive's larger purpose was to undermine the American will to fight. North Vietnam believed it could demonstrate to American war leaders that they could not win in Vietnam by military means. American war leaders had been taking steps to convince the American public and news media that the enemy was almost defeated. The Tet Offensive was designed to prove this statement false and convince the United States that it should negotiate an end to the war.

Despite much heavy fighting, the Communists failed to achieve these objectives. No widespread uprising of the population occurred in South Vietnam. In addition, the United States and South Vietnam quickly recovered their early losses, and the enemy suffered a huge number of

The Tet Offensive was a yearlong assault on South Vietnamese targets during the Vietnam War. Prior to the Tet Offensive, many American war leaders claimed that the Communists were nearly defeated. In 1968, Communist North Vietnamese and Viet Cong soldiers launched a series of attacks on such major cities as Saigon and Hue. The Tet Offensive convinced many Americans that the war was likely to be long and costly, with no outright victory for either side.

casualties. But the Tet attacks stunned the American people and demoralized their war managers. Shortly before the Tet Offensive, the U.S. commander in the field, General William C. Westmoreland, had assured the nation that the enemy had already been largely beaten. But the Tet Offensive seemed to contradict this statement. As a result of the Tet Offensive, U.S. President Lyndon B. Johnson made a number of basic changes in his policies. Johnson cut back the bombing of North Vietnam and rejected Westmoreland's request for 206,000 additional troops. Johnson also called for peace negotiations and declared that he would not seek re-election in 1968. Clark Clifford (1906-1998), who was the U.S.

defense secretary from March 1968 to January 1969, led a group of officials who persuaded Johnson to de-escalate the Vietnam War. Clifford argued that the burden of fighting in the war should be transferred from U.S. troops to South Vietnamese forces. Peace talks opened in Paris in May.

The peace talks failed to produce an agreement, and many more Americans became impatient for the war to end. U.S. President Richard M. Nixon, who was elected president in 1968, felt he had to reduce U.S. involvement in Vietnam. On June 8, 1969, he announced a new policy known as Vietnamization. This policy called for stepped-up training programs for South Vietnamese forces and the gradual withdrawal of U.S. troops from Vietnam. The U.S. troop withdrawal began in July 1969. Also that year, U.S. planes began to bomb Communist targets in Cambodia. During the 1950's and 1960's, Cambodia had declared itself neutral in the struggle between Communist and non-Communist nations. But Cambodian King Norodom Sihanouk (*NAWR uh dum SEE uh nuk*) (1922-2012) secretly allowed North Vietnamese Communists—the enemies of the United States and South Vietnam—to establish bases in Cambodia. Sihanouk gave up the throne in 1955 and was elected prime minister. He was elected head of state in 1960.

In April 1970, Nixon ordered United States and South Vietnamese troops to clear out military supply centers that North Vietnam had set up in Cambodia. Large stocks of weapons were captured, and the invasion may have delayed a major enemy attack. The United States troops left Cambodia at the end of June, but the Vietnamese Communists had withdrawn deeper into Cambodia. By the end of 1970, all of Cambodia was at war. Government forces fought the Communists with the help of South Vietnamese troops and U.S. military aid. Also, that year, the prime minister, Lieutenant General Lon Nol (*lahn nohl*) (1913-1985), and

Prince Sisowath Sirik Matak (*see rihk mah tahk*) ousted Sihanouk and forced him into exile.

Growing protest

Many Americans felt the Cambodia campaign widened the war. The invasion of Cambodia aroused a storm of protest in the United States, especially on college and university campuses.

The nation was shocked on May 4, 1970, when Ohio National Guard units fired into a group of students protesting the Vietnam War at Kent State University. The shots killed four students and wounded nine others. Antiwar demonstrations and riots occurred on hundreds of campuses throughout May. A move began in Congress to force the removal of troops from Cambodia. On June 3, Nixon announced the completion of troop withdrawal. That same day, the Senate voted to repeal the Tonkin Gulf Resolution. These actions ended the Cambodian campaign.

Opposition to the war in the United States grew rapidly during Nixon's presidency. John Kerry (1943-   ), who was wounded in combat in Vietnam and received three Purple Heart citations and Silver Star and Bronze Star medals during his tour in the Navy from 1966 to 1970, helped found Vietnam Veterans of America. Kerry became a leader and spokesperson for the antiwar group Vietnam Veterans Against the War after returning from service. Many people claimed that this increased opposition was due to the news media, particularly television coverage, which brought scenes of the war into millions of homes. However, most scholars have concluded that media coverage reflected, rather than brought about, America's growing opposition to the war.

In March 1971, the conviction of Lieutenant William L. Calley, Jr., for war crimes raised some of the main moral issues of the conflict. Calley's unit was part of the Army company that massacred hundreds of civil-

A mass protest against the Vietnam War turned violent at Kent State University in 1970. Ohio National Guard units fired into the crowd of student protesters, killing four and wounding nine others.

ians in 1968 in the hamlet of My Lai (*mee ly*) in South Vietnam. The My Lai massacre caused Americans' support for the war effort to drop, at a time when support was already low.

On March 16, 1968, at the height of the war, U.S. Army troops entered the small South Vietnamese community of My Lai in search of enemy forces. In past weeks, there had been many U.S. casualties in the area. The troops found only unarmed women, children, and old men in My Lai. The soldiers, who were partly under Calley's command, rounded up and then shot and killed hundreds of the civilians. The soldiers first tortured or raped some of them. None of the civilians had offered any

Conscientious objector

A conscientious objector is a person who claims that his or her beliefs prevent them from bearing arms in their country's armed forces. A conscientious objector may be willing to serve in the military, but only as a noncombatant, such as a member of a medical corps. Or they may claim that their principles do not allow them to take part in any effort associated with war. Of the major countries, the United States and the United Kingdom were the first to consistently accept conscientious objection in exempting people from military service or combat training.

The history of conscientious objection in the United States dates back to colonial times, when men had to serve in their colony's militia. The first conscientious objectors in America were members of pacifist religious groups, such as the Quakers.

In 1661, Massachusetts became the first colony to exempt conscientious objectors from service in its militia. Congress passed the first federal draft law during the Civil War (1861-1865). This law recognized conscientious objectors, and they received special consideration in both the North and the South. To be classified as a conscientious objector, a man had to belong to a pacifist religious group. This requirement was also followed during World War I (1914-1918). Men classified as conscientious objectors were excused from combat, but were expected to perform some sort of military service.

The 1940 draft law required "religious training and belief," but not necessarily membership in a pacifist religious group, for conscientious objection. The 1948 draft law defined religious belief as belief in a "Supreme Being." But Congress removed the

In 1967, world heavyweight boxing champion Muhammad Ali refused to serve in the Vietnam War, saying he was a conscientious objector. Ali was later convicted for refusing induction into the army and sentenced to prison. He was also stripped of his boxing title.

term "Supreme Being" in the 1967 law because the U.S. Supreme Court interpreted the term to include vaguely religious philosophies. From 1967 to 1970, exemptions were granted chiefly to people whose "religious training and belief" led them to believe all war is wrong.

The religious requirement was strongly questioned during the 1960's. Many men sought exemptions on the basis of their personal philosophy or their belief that the Vietnam War (1957-1975) was immoral. Major churches came to support selective objection—the refusal to serve in a particular war. In 1970, the Supreme Court exempted from military service "all those whose consciences, spurred by deeply held moral, ethical, or religious beliefs, would give them no rest or peace if they allowed themselves to become part of an instrument of war." Many countries provide alternative forms of national service for objectors in an effort to reconcile the claims of national security and individual conscience.

The fighting intensifies

U.S. Army Lieutenant William L. Calley, Jr., (right) was found guilty of war crimes during the Vietnam War in what became known as the My Lai Massacre. U.S. troops partly under his command rounded up and killed hundreds of civilians in the small hamlet of My Lai in South Vietnam.

resistance to the U.S. forces.

The U.S. military tried to cover up the massacre, but information about it became public in November 1969. Although 25 men were charged with crimes, only Calley was found guilty of the murder of at least 22 Vietnamese. He was sentenced to life in prison. He was then paroled in 1974 after his sentence was repeatedly reduced.

Some Americans said Calley was unfairly singled out, arguing that Vietnam combat was so stressful that cruelty was inevitable. Some war critics used Calley's trial to call attention to the large numbers of civilians killed by U.S. bombing and ground operations in South Vietnam.

Others pointed to the vast stretches of countryside that had been destroyed by bombing and the spraying of chemicals.

One type of bomb the United States used was made from napalm (*NAY pahm*), a powder used to thicken gasoline for use in war. When napalm is added to gasoline, the result is a jellylike explosive, which is also called napalm. When a napalm bomb is dropped from the air, it bursts, ignites, and splatters burning napalm over a wide area. The jellied

The U.S. military has used napalm as a weapon of war since World War II (1939-1945). This photo shows a napalm bomb erupting into a fireball on Viet Cong structures in South Vietnam during the Vietnam War.

The fighting intensifies

gasoline clings to everything it touches and burns violently. Napalm causes death from burns or suffocation.

Napalm is also used in flame throwers carried by ground troops. A flame thrower is a device that shoots a stream of burning fuel, much as a fire hose shoots water. A flexible tube connects the flame gun to fuel tanks on the operator's back. A tank of compressed air between the fuel tanks provides the pressure to squirt the fuel through the gun. Portable flame throwers weigh a total of about 50 pounds (23 kilograms) when they are ready to fire.

In the 1960's and early 1970's, the United States armed forces also used a weedkiller called Agent Orange as a weapon in the Vietnam war. U.S. forces sprayed Agent Orange over jungles and farms in South Vietnam and Laos. Agent Orange was used to *defoliate* (cause the leaves to fall off) trees, shrubs, and other plants to reveal enemy hiding places in the jungle and to destroy enemy food crops. Agent Orange consisted of mainly two plant-killing compounds called 2,4-D and 2,4,5-T. It also contained a type of compound called a *dioxin*.

Some veterans of the war blamed Agent Orange for their health problems. In 1990, the Centers for Disease Control (now the Centers for Disease Control and Prevention), a U.S. government agency, released a study of Agent Orange. The study found no evidence that Agent Orange increased the risk of cancer among Vietnam veterans. That same year, a congressional committee declared the study flawed. In 1991, Congress passed a bill providing disability benefits for Vietnam veterans suffering from certain illnesses believed caused by Agent Orange.

In 1993, the Institute of Medicine (now the National Academy of Medicine), an adviser to the U.S. government, released another study of Agent Orange. It linked exposure to Agent Orange to three kinds of cancer and two skin diseases. The study reached these conclusions

During the Vietnam War, U.S. troops used the weedkiller Agent Orange to defoliate trees, shrubs, and other plants to reveal enemy hiding places in the Vietnamese jungle and to destroy enemy food crops. This photo shows U.S. military planes spraying Agent Orange over Vietnam in 1966. Some Vietnam War veterans blamed Agent Orange for their health problems.

based on civilians' exposure on the job. It recommended additional studies to determine the effects of Agent Orange on veterans.

Pentagon Papers

Public distrust of the U.S. government deepened in June 1971, when newspapers published a secret government study of the war called the *Pentagon Papers.* This study raised questions about decisions and secret actions of government leaders regarding the war.

The *Pentagon Papers* was a U.S. Department of Defense secret study of U.S. involvement in Vietnam from the 1940's to early 1968. The papers were first made public in *The New York Times* in June 1971, during the

In 1971, newspapers published a secret U.S. Department of Defense study of the Vietnam War called the *Pentagon Papers* (shown at right). The study raised questions about decisions and secret actions of U.S. government and military leaders regarding the war. The study also revealed how the administrations of four U.S. presidents had all misled the public regarding U.S. involvement in Vietnam.

Vietnam War. The Supreme Court of the United States blocked the government's attempt to prevent the study's publication. The court decision was widely regarded as a powerful demonstration of the openness of U.S. society. The document's official title was *Report of the Office of the Secretary of Defense Vietnam Task Force*. It was called the *Pentagon Papers* after the Pentagon Building, which houses the Department of Defense headquarters.

During the late 1960's and early 1970's, public opposition to America's involvement in Vietnam became widespread throughout the United States. In 1971, Daniel Ellsberg (1931-   ), a military analyst who had worked on the *Pentagon Papers*, copied the document and leaked it to *The New York Times*. (To *leak* information is to pass the information stealthily or indirectly.) Ellsberg had come to believe that the war was wrong and unjust, and he hoped the release of the study would hasten the war's end. He also felt compelled to disclose what he considered to be the illegal and unconstitutional actions of high-ranking members of the U.S. government and military.

The first *Pentagon Papers* article appeared in *The New York Times* on June 13, 1971. Two days later, the U.S. Department of Justice obtained a temporary restraining order to stop *The New York Times* from publishing further related articles while the government sought a permanent injunction against publication. The newspaper appealed the case, called the *New York Times Co. v. United States*, to the U.S. Supreme Court. On June 18, *The Washington Post* also began publishing articles based on the *Pentagon Papers*, resulting in another restraining order and appeal. The Supreme Court heard both appeals jointly.

On June 30, the Supreme Court held, in a 6-3 decision, that the government failed to justify restraint of publication. The court forbade such prior censorship of the press unless it was justified by an emergency and

On June 30, 1971, the U.S. Supreme Court ruled against the Nixon administration's effort to block publication of the top-secret *Pentagon Papers*. Following the ruling, U.S. Senator Birch Evans Bayh, Jr., of Indiana (above) addressed reporters in front of the Supreme Court Building in Washington, D.C. Bayh won national attention in the 1960's for his opposition to U.S. involvement in Vietnam.

could be linked to "direct, immediate, and irreparable harm" to the nation. Citing freedom of the press, which is guaranteed by the First Amendment to the Constitution of the United States, the court allowed the newspapers to continue publishing articles on the *Pentagon Papers*.

The Department of Justice charged Ellsberg and fellow analyst Anthony J. Russo, Jr., who had assisted Ellsberg, with conspiracy, theft, and espionage for releasing classified documents. In 1973, the charges against Ellsberg and Russo were dropped after revelations of improper actions taken by the administration of President Richard Nixon and numerous irregularities in the government's case. The administration's improper actions included a break-in at the office of Ellsberg's psychiatrist by a secret investigative unit formed by Nixon known as the *Plumbers*. The Plumbers later became involved in events that led to the Watergate scandal, which resulted in Nixon's resignation.

In 1967, U.S. Secretary of Defense Robert McNamara (1916-2009) commissioned the *Pentagon Papers* as an official history of the Vietnam War. About 7,000 pages long, the papers revealed that the main reason for U.S. involvement in Vietnam was to prevent the influence of Communist China from spreading throughout Southeast Asia. The papers also showed how the U.S. military had concealed from Congress that it had expanded the war effort in Southeast Asia by bombing Cambodia and Laos and raiding the North Vietnamese coast. They also illustrated how the presidential administrations of Harry S. Truman, Dwight D. Eisenhower, John F. Kennedy, and Lyndon B. Johnson had all misled the public regarding U.S. involvement in Vietnam. The papers further enraged an agitated U.S. public, but they had little effect on the war in Vietnam, which continued until 1975. Some parts of the *Pentagon Papers*, however, were not leaked. These sections remained classified until 2011, when the government declassified and released the complete report.

The Paris Peace Accords ended U.S. military involvement in the Vietnam War. Representatives from 12 nations and the United Nations (shown here) met in Paris, France, in January 1973, to sign the treaties, which called for the end of all hostilities and the withdrawal of U.S. and other foreign ground troops from Vietnam. North Vietnam ignored the treaties and resumed its invasion of South Vietnam. The South Vietnamese surrendered in 1975.

U.S. President Dwight D. Eisenhower (left) greeted South Vietnamese President Ngo Dinh Diem at Washington National Airport during a visit to the United States in 1957. Eisenhower provided economic aid and military advisers to assist Diem in setting up a non-Communist government after the division of Vietnam.

In March 1972, North Vietnam began a major invasion of South Vietnam. Nixon then renewed the bombing of North Vietnam and used American airpower against the exposed formations of regular enemy troops and tanks. Nixon also ordered the placing of explosives in the harbor of Haiphong, which is near the Gulf of Tonkin and served as North Vietnam's major port for importing military supplies. This helped stop the invasion, which had nearly reached the South Vietnamese capital, Saigon, by August 1972.

In October 1963, President John F. Kennedy (right) met with his advisers—Secretary of Defense Robert S. McNamara (1916-2009) (center) and General Maxwell D. Taylor (1901-1987), chairman of the Joint Chiefs of Staff—about their trip to South Vietnam. McNamara promoted increasing U.S. involvement in Vietnam.

After several years of intense fighting in Vietnam, the United States was unable to sustain its participation in the war. Public opposition to the war had intensified from the late 1960's to the early 1970's. Nixon's policy of Vietnamization shifted the burden of fighting to South Vietnam, although too slowly to satisfy many war critics. The Cambodia campaign and the My Lai Massacre raised further questions about the U.S. involvement. Further peace talks would bring removal of U.S. troops, and eventually the end of the war.

The fighting intensifies

Lyndon B. Johnson served as president of the United States from Nov. 22, 1963, until 1969. The widening war in Vietnam became Johnson's chief problem.

CHAPTER FOUR

U.S. presidents, personalities, and leaders of the war

Lyndon B. Johnson

United States Vice President Lyndon Baines Johnson (1908-1973) became president on Nov. 22, 1963, following the fatal shooting of President John F. Kennedy in a motorcade in Dallas, Texas.

Johnson had served in Congress for almost 24 years before he was elected vice president in 1960. In 1937, at the age of 29, he won election to the U.S. House of Representatives. He was elected to the U.S. Senate in 1948. Five years later, at the age of 44, he was made Senate Democratic leader—the youngest person up to that time ever elected to lead either party in the Senate.

Johnson led the Democratic-controlled Senate during the administration of Republican President Dwight D. Eisenhower. Johnson was powerful and shrewdly mixed the demands of party politics with a sense of cooperation between Democrats and Republicans. He frequently brought about agreement through clever planning and persuasion. As president, his image as a master politician caused many people to mistrust him.

Johnson's skill in congressional politics was not enough to overcome the problems raised by the Vietnam War. His failure to explain the deepening U.S. involvement in the war cost him much support and led to a national debate that proved disastrous to his political position.

With over half a million U.S. troops in Vietnam in what appeared to be an endless struggle, disagreement at home increased.

Johnson conferred with many of the world leaders who came to Kennedy's funeral. He stated his basic foreign policy on Nov. 27, 1963: "This nation will keep its commitments from South Vietnam to West Berlin. We will be unceasing in the search for peace; resourceful in our pursuit of areas of agreement even with those with whom we differ; and generous and loyal to those who join with us in common cause."

In 1964, President Johnson easily won nomination for his first full term. He was nominated on his 56th birthday. He chose Senator Hubert H. Humphrey of Minnesota as his running mate. Their Republican opponents were Senator Barry M. Goldwater of Arizona and Representative William E. Miller of New York.

Johnson won reelection in a landslide. He received 486 electoral votes to only 52 for Senator Goldwater, and Johnson carried 44 states and the District of Columbia.

The widening Vietnam War became Johnson's chief problem. When he became president, U.S. forces in Vietnam comprised about 16,300 military advisers. In the spring and summer of 1965, he ordered the first U.S. combat troops into South Vietnam to protect U.S. bases there and to stop the Communists from overrunning the country. U.S. planes stepped up bombing attacks against North Vietnam. The number of casualties and the cost of the war mounted. By 1968, there were more than 500,000 U.S. troops in South Vietnam.

A bitter debate developed in the United States over the U.S. role in the war. Many Americans became *hawks,* favoring sterner military action to end the war. Many others became *doves,* calling for a cutback in the fighting and eventual U.S. withdrawal from the war. Two of the chief critics of U.S. involvement in the war were Democratic Senators Eugene

United States President Lyndon B. Johnson shook hands with American troops during a visit to South Vietnam in 1966. In 1965, Johnson had ordered the first U.S. combat troops into South Vietnam and stepped up the bombing of North Vietnam.

McCarthy of Minnesota and Robert F. Kennedy of New York.

Johnson took part in several conferences with other world leaders. In October 1966, he discussed the Vietnam War with six Asian allied leaders in Manila, in the Philippines. In June 1967, he met Soviet Premier Aleksei Kosygin (*ah lehk SAY ko SEE gihn*) (1904-1980) in Glassboro, New Jersey, to discuss world problems.

Opposition grew to the increasing U.S. role in the Vietnam War, and racial unrest increased. Demonstrations occurred throughout the nation. Riots broke out in the overcrowded slums of Chicago, Cleveland,

In October 1966, U.S. President Lyndon B. Johnson (far right) met with Asian allied leaders in the capital city of Manila, in the Philippines, to discuss the Vietnam War.

Detroit, Los Angeles, New York City, and Newark. Johnson had to send federal troops to Detroit in July 1967 to stop a riot there. He appointed a special commission of prominent Americans headed by Illinois Governor Otto Kerner to try to determine causes of the riots. The commission warned that the United States was moving toward two societies, "one black, one white—separate but unequal."

Johnson shocked the nation by announcing on March 31, 1968, that he would not run for reelection. The president said there was "division in the American house" and that he was withdrawing in the name of national unity. At the same time, he announced a reduction in bombing of North Vietnam.

Johnson's order to reduce bombing led to talks between U.S. and North

Vietnamese representatives. The talks started in Paris on May 13, 1968. Johnson halted all bombing and other U.S. attacks on North Vietnamese territory on Nov. 1, 1968. Johnson's action led to peace talks involving the governments of the United States, North Vietnam, and South Vietnam, and a delegation from the Communist-led National Liberation Front.

Richard Nixon

Richard Milhous Nixon (1913-1994) was the only president of the United States ever to resign from office. He left the presidency on Aug. 9, 1974, while facing certain impeachment for his involvement in the Watergate scandal. (*Impeachment* is the formal accusation of serious misconduct against a government official.) The Watergate scandal included a break-in at the national headquarters of the Democratic Party and other illegal activities by employees of Nixon's 1972 reelection committee and members of his executive staff. Nixon's attempts to cover up these crimes became a major part of the scandal.

Although Nixon left office in disgrace, he had won respect for his conduct of foreign policy. As president, he ended U.S. military participation in Vietnam in 1973 and eased the tension that had existed for years between the United States and both China and the Soviet Union. Nixon became the first president to visit China while in office. He also visited the Soviet Union. He won congressional approval of U.S.-Soviet trade agreements and agreements to limit the production of nuclear weapons.

In February 1968, Nixon announced that he would be a candidate for the Republican presidential nomination. Many Republicans wondered whether he could regain his voter appeal. They feared that his defeats by Kennedy in the 1960 presidential election and Edmund G. (Pat) Brown in the 1962 California gubernatorial election had given him the image of a

President Richard M. Nixon was the only U.S. president ever to resign from office. As president, Nixon's major goal was settlement of the Vietnam War. In 1973, he ended U.S. military participation in the war.

loser. But Nixon won primary elections by large margins in New Hampshire, Wisconsin, Indiana, Nebraska, Oregon, and South Dakota.

Nixon's chief opponents for the presidential nomination were Governors Nelson Rockefeller of New York and Ronald Reagan of California. But Nixon easily won nomination on the first ballot at the Republican National Convention in Miami Beach, Florida. The convention nominated Nixon's choice as running mate, Governor Spiro T. Agnew of Maryland.

The Democrats chose Vice President Hubert H. Humphrey and Senator Edmund S. Muskie of Maine.

Both Nixon and Humphrey promised to make peace in Vietnam their main goal as president. The Vietnam War had begun in 1957 as a battle for control of South Vietnam between South Vietnam's non-Communist government and Communist-backed South Vietnamese rebels called the Viet Cong. By the mid-1960's, the United States was deeply involved in the war as an ally of the South Vietnamese government.

Nixon called for a program of what he termed "new internationalism." Under the plan, other nations would take over from the United States more of the responsibility for preserving world peace and helping developing countries. This plan later became known as the Nixon Doctrine.

In the election, Nixon defeated Humphrey by only about 511,000 popular votes, 31,785,148 to 31,274,503. Nixon won a clear majority of electoral votes, with 301. Humphrey received 191 electoral votes.

Nixon's major goal was settlement of the Vietnam War. In his first inaugural address, Nixon said: "The greatest honor history can bestow is the title of peacemaker. This honor now beckons America."

The Vietnam peace talks, begun in 1968, continued in Paris. But the negotiators made little progress. In March 1969, Nixon ordered a stepped-up training program for South Vietnamese forces so they could gradually take on the major burden of fighting. He also ordered secret bombings of supply routes in Cambodia. In July, he began a gradual withdrawal of U.S. combat troops from Vietnam, a policy known as *Vietnamization.* Many Americans favored it, but many others wanted U.S. involvement to end immediately. Protests and demonstrations swept the nation.

In 1970, United States troops invaded Cambodia to attack North Vietnamese supply depots there. Nixon said the action would shorten the war, but many people felt it was expanding it. Protests broke out on hundreds of college campuses. At Kent State University in Ohio, National Guardsmen fired into a crowd of demonstrators, killing four students and wounding nine others. The shocked reaction of the nation and student strikes at other colleges, many of which closed until fall, forced Nixon to cut short the Cambodian campaign.

In May 1972, in response to a Communist offensive, Nixon ordered a blockade of North Vietnam to cut off its war supplies from the Soviet Union and China. The blockade included the mining of North Vietnam's ports and the bombing of its rail and highway links to China. In December 1972, after peace negotiations broke down, Nixon ordered extensive bombing of Hanoi, the North Vietnamese capital.

Nixon and Agnew easily won renomination at the 1972 Republican National Convention in Miami Beach. The Democrats nominated Senator George S. McGovern of South Dakota for president. Sargent Shriver, former director of the Peace Corps, became McGovern's running mate.

In the election, Nixon won a landslide victory. He received almost 18 million more popular votes than McGovern—the widest margin of any U.S. presidential election. Nixon got 520 electoral votes, and McGovern received 17.

On Jan. 27, 1973, the United States and the other participants in the

Richard M. Nixon makes his trademark "V for victory" sign while campaigning for president of the United States in 1968. Nixon defeated the Democratic candidate Vice President Hubert H. Humphrey in the presidential election. In response to a Communist offensive in the Vietnam War, Nixon ordered a blockade of North Vietnam to cut off its war supplies from the Soviet Union and China. When peace negotiations broke down, he ordered extensive bombing of Hanoi, the North Vietnamese capital.

Vietnam War signed agreements to stop fighting immediately and begin exchanging prisoners. The agreements climaxed several weeks of bargaining between North Vietnamese officials and Henry A. Kissinger (1923-   ), Nixon's national security adviser, who had begun secret talks with the Communists in 1969. The United States completed its troop withdrawal from South Vietnam in March. Nixon privately assured South Vietnam that the United States would use "full force" to aid the South Vietnamese if the Communists violated the agreements. Fighting did continue in 1973, but no U.S. troops reentered the war.

On Jan. 23, 1973, U.S. President Richard M. Nixon announced the preliminary approval of the Paris Peace Accords, ending U.S. involvement in the Vietnam War. Four days later, on Jan. 27, a cease-fire agreement was signed in Paris, France, by the United States, South Vietnam, North Vietnam, and the Viet Cong. The pact provided for the withdrawal of all U.S. and allied forces from Vietnam and the return of all prisoners of war—both within 60 days.

Later that year, Kissinger became secretary of state.

Nixon continued his efforts to improve relations between the United States and China. In 1973, the two nations sent representatives to serve in each other's capital and exchanged visits by cultural groups.

The president suffered a major defeat when Congress forced him to end U.S. bombing in Cambodia. Nixon had argued that the bombing was needed to prevent a Communist takeover of that nation. But Congress refused to provide money for bombing beyond Aug. 15, 1973.

Nixon received another major setback in 1973 when Congress overrode his veto of a resolution that limited presidential war powers. The War Powers Resolution gives Congress the power to halt after 60 days the use of any U.S. armed forces that the president has ordered into combat abroad. Passage of the resolution was the strongest action ever taken by Congress to spell out the warmaking powers of Congress and the president.

Daniel and Philip Berrigan

Daniel and Philip Berrigan were American Roman Catholic priests who became known for their social and political activism. Daniel (1921-2016) and Philip (1923-2002) dedicated much of their lives to the causes of social justice and pacifism (the opposition to war or violence), especially opposition to the Vietnam War and nuclear arms. The brothers' acts of protest and civil disobedience resulted in numerous arrests and years spent in prison. They also sparked a wave of protests by others.

The Berrigans may be most famous as members of the "Catonsville Nine." On May 17, 1968, Daniel, Philip, and seven other Vietnam War protesters took hundreds of draft records from a local draft board office in Catonsville, Maryland, and burned them publicly. The Berrigans were convicted of conspiracy and destroying government property and sentenced to prison. They went into hiding before they were due to report to prison. However, they eventually were caught and served part of their sentences before being released. Throughout their lives, the Berrigans carried out many similar attacks on government property and defense-related sites. For example, in 1980, they raided a General Electric plant in King of Prussia, a suburb of Philadelphia, Pennsylvania, where they used hammers to damage missile warheads. The brothers also founded a number of pacifist groups, including the Catholic Peace Fellowship.

Daniel Joseph Berrigan was born on May 9, 1921, in Virginia, Minnesota. Philip Francis Berrigan was born on Oct. 5, 1923, in Two Harbors, Minnesota. Their father, a political radical and labor organizer, may have influenced his sons to become activists. The boys grew up on a farm in Syracuse, New York.

Daniel attended St. Andrew-on-Hudson, a Jesuit seminary in Hyde Park, New York, where he received a bachelor's degree in 1946. In 1952, he received a master's degree from Woodstock College in Baltimore, Maryland. That same year, he was ordained as a priest. In 1953, he traveled to France, where he was influenced by the Worker Priests movement, in which priests took jobs as laborers to better understand the working class. Later travels to Europe, Latin America, South Africa, and Vietnam further shaped Daniel's social and political views.

Beginning in the 1940's, Daniel pursued a career of teaching and writing. He taught at Catholic preparatory schools in New Jersey and New York. He also held positions at several colleges and universities, including Le Moyne College in Syracuse, New York; Loyola University New Orleans in Louisiana; Columbia and Fordham universities in New York City, New York; Cornell University in Ithaca, New York; and Yale University in New Haven, Connecticut.

Daniel Berrigan (left) and his brother Philip (center) were American Roman Catholic priests who became known for their social and political activism against war, especially the Vietnam War, and social injustice in the 1960's and 1970's. They were arrested many times for acts of protest. This picture shows the brothers with a U.S. marshal at the U.S. District Court in Hartford, Connecticut, in 1970.

On May 17, 1968, Roman Catholic priests Philip Berrigan (center) and Daniel Berrigan (right) were Vietnam War protesters who, along with seven others, became known as the "Catonsville Nine." The group took hundreds of draft records from a local draft board office in Catonsville, Maryland, and burned them publicly. Throughout their lives, the Berrigan brothers carried out many similar attacks on government property and defense-related sites.

Daniel wrote more than 50 books, including works of poetry, social and religious criticism, and Biblical commentary. For many years, he traveled throughout the United States speaking on social and political issues. In the 1980's, he worked as a hospital chaplain in New York City, ministering to cancer and AIDS patients. In 1997, Daniel was nominated for the Nobel Peace Prize. Daniel died on April 30, 2016, in New York City.

Philip was drafted into the United States Army in 1943 and served in Europe during World War II. During his military service, he was strongly influenced by the discrimination he witnessed against African Americans. Philip received a bachelor's degree in literature from the College of the Holy Cross in Worcester, Massachusetts, in 1950. He received a second bachelor's degree, in secondary education, from Loyola University New Orleans in 1957, and a master's degree in education from Xavier University of Louisiana in 1960. In 1955, he was ordained as a member of the Josephite Fathers, an order dedicated to helping African Americans. Philip then served as a priest and teacher in New Orleans; Newburgh, New York; and Baltimore, often working with poor African Americans.

In 1969, Philip and Elizabeth McAlister, a nun in the antiwar movement, secretly declared themselves married. The couple legalized their marriage in 1973 and were excommunicated from the Catholic Church. Individuals who are excommunicated from the Catholic Church are forbidden from participating in any of the religion's ceremonies. They settled in Baltimore, where they established Jonah House, a communal home for pacifists. In 1980, Philip helped establish the antinuclear Plowshares movement. Philip also wrote a number of books about pacifism and social justice. He died on Dec. 6, 2002, in Baltimore.

Jane Fonda

Jane Fonda (1937-   ) is an American motion-picture actress. She has appeared in more than 45 films, many of which she co-produced through her own company. Fonda won Academy Awards as best actress for her performances in *Klute* (1971) and *Coming Home* (1978).

Jane Seymour Fonda was born on Dec. 21, 1937, in New York City. She is the daughter of the actor Henry Fonda. She made her film debut in *Tall Story* (1960). Her other films include *A Walk on the Wild Side* (1962); *Cat Ballou* (1965); *Barbarella* (1968); *They Shoot Horses, Don't They?* (1969); *Julia* (1977); *The China Syndrome* (1979); *On Golden Pond* (1981), in which she co-starred with her father; *The Morning After* (1987); *Stanley and Iris*

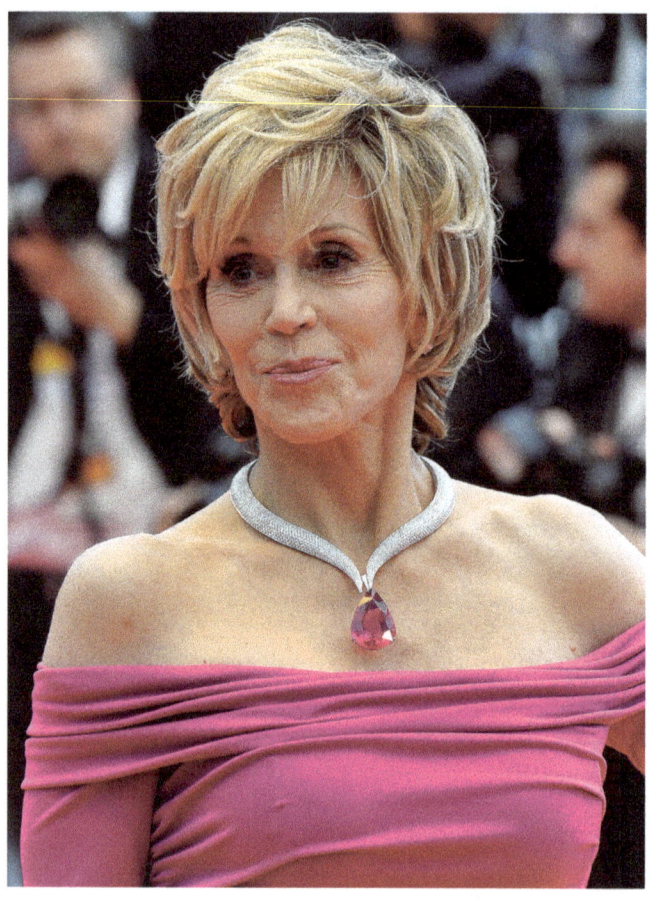

Jane Fonda is an American motion-picture actress, who also became noted for her anti-Vietnam War views. She won Academy Awards as best actress for her performances in *Klute* (1971) and *Coming Home* (1978).

(1990); *Monster-in-Law* (2005); *Peace, Love, and Misunderstanding* (2012); Lee Daniels' *The Butler* (2013); *This Is Where I Leave You* (2014); and *Youth* (2015).

Fonda became noted for her antiwar views during American participation in the Vietnam War from 1965 to 1973 and for her work as a political activist. In July 1972, Fonda traveled to North Vietnam to observe, firsthand, the effects of U.S. bombing. While there, she made daily broadcasts to American servicemen over North Vietnam's propaganda radio station Radio Hanoi. Although several U.S. Congressmen

Actress Jane Fonda (right) meets with U.S. prisoners of war in North Vietnam during a visit there in 1972. Fonda earned the nickname "Hanoi Jane" for her daily antiwar broadcasts to American servicemen over Radio Hanoi. Several U.S. Congressmen accused her of treason.

accused her of treason and of undermining the morale of American servicemen, she continued to speak out against the war. In late 1970, Fonda had begun lecturing against the war throughout the United States and donating the proceeds to Vietnam Veterans Against the War. She also led a 15-member troupe in presenting a "Free the Army" show near U.S. military bases.

Fonda was married to French motion-picture director Roger Vadim from 1965 to 1973, American political activist and politician Tom Hayden from 1973 to 1990, and American broadcasting executive Ted Turner from 1991 to 2001. Her brother, Peter Fonda, is also an actor. She wrote an autobiography, *My Life So Far* (2005), and a memoir and self-help book, *Prime Time* (2011). In 2015, she began acting in the Netflix comedy series "Grace and Frankie."

Le Duc Tho

Le Duc Tho (*lay duhk tow*) (1911-1990), a top-ranking Vietnamese Communist Party official and representative of what was then the government of North Vietnam, became the first Asian and the first member of a Communist government to receive a Nobel Prize for peace. He shared the peace prize in 1973 with United States Secretary of State Henry A. Kissinger. The two men were awarded the prize after taking part in long and difficult negotiations to bring about a cease-fire in the Vietnam War. But the award proved controversial. Many people resented its being given to Le Duc Tho because of his record as a Communist actively involved in the Indochina conflicts of the mid-1900's. Le Duc Tho himself pointed out that the cease-fire did not mark the end of the war in Vietnam and therefore refused his share of the peace prize.

Little is known for certain about the early life of Le Duc Tho. According to an official biographical sketch issued in 1973, he was born in the village of Dich Le (*zihk lay*), in Nam Ha province, Vietnam. His real name was apparently Phan Dinh Khai (*fan din hy*). His father is said to have been a middle-ranking civil servant in the French colonial administration. By 1930, Le Duc Tho had committed himself to the struggle for Vietnamese independence from French rule. While working in the postal service as a radiotelegrapher, he organized demonstrations and

Henry A. Kissinger (right), chief foreign policy adviser to U.S. President Richard M. Nixon, shake hands with Le Duc Tho, the chief North Vietnamese negotiator, after negotiating the Paris Peace Accords in the French capital in January 1973. Kissinger and Le Duc Tho shared the 1973 Nobel Peace Prize for their role in the cease-fire that ended the Vietnam War.

riots against the French and worked with Ho Chi Minh and other youthful revolutionaries in setting up the Indochinese Communist Party. For his anti-French actions, he was imprisoned in a forced labor camp on the island of Poulo Condor (now known as Con Son). After his release in 1936, he immediately resumed his political work, leading a Communist propaganda organization in the city of Nam Dinh. The French authorities imprisoned him again in 1939, but it is unclear how he spent the years of World War II (1939-1945). His official biography says that he was held in prison until 1944. Other sources report that he escaped from prison in 1940 and fled to China, where he helped Ho Chi Minh found the *Vietminh,* a Communist nationalist organization.

By mid-1945, Le Duc Tho was living in Hanoi, in northern Vietnam, and was a member of the central committee and the standing committee of the Indochinese Communist Party. During the war of liberation against the French, he was sent to the south of the country, where he helped establish the Vietnamese Communist Party's Central Office for South Vietnam. In 1954, under an agreement signed in Geneva, the French finally left Vietnam. Pending democratic elections, Vietnam was temporarily divided into South Vietnam, governed by a pro-Western regime in Saigon (now Ho Chi Minh City) and North Vietnam, ruled by a Communist government in Hanoi, headed by Ho Chi Minh. In 1955, Le Duc Tho moved to North Vietnam and became a member of the Communist Party's *politburo* (chief ruling political body). In 1956, he visited Moscow as a representative of the North Vietnamese government. In 1960, he became secretary of the Central Committee.

The elections promised under the Geneva agreement failed to take place by 1956, and the South Vietnamese Communists, whose guerrilla forces became known as the *Viet Cong,* launched a military campaign to unify the country under Communist rule. The North Vietnamese government backed the Viet Cong against the South Vietnamese army. This civil war gradually broadened into the Vietnam War of the 1960's and early 1970's, in which the United States became increasingly involved. Le Duc Tho was a hard-line supporter of the war against South Vietnam. He supervised North Vietnam's secret control of the Viet Cong's activities.

In 1968, cease-fire negotiations opened in Paris between the United States and North Vietnam. Le Duc Tho was officially an adviser to the North Vietnamese delegation, but in reality, as a high-ranking member of the Politburo, he was the chief negotiator. The public talks faltered and became bogged down, but in 1969 Le Duc Tho and United States foreign policy adviser Henry Kissinger began secret discussions. Le Duc Tho proved a tough, but courteous and authoritative negotiator. His meetings with Kissinger made slow but steady progress. In 1972, U.S. President Richard Nixon made the secret talks public. Eventually, a cease-fire agreement was hammered out and signed on Jan. 27, 1973. Under the agreement, all American troops withdrew from Vietnam by April 1973.

The cease-fire remained largely unobserved on both sides, and fighting continued. Le Duc Tho was present in South Vietnam during the concluding offensive against the Saigon-based regime, which finally surrendered in April 1975. In 1982, he expressed his support for economic reform in Vietnam. He was reportedly ranked fourth in the Vietnamese Communist Party hierarchy when he retired from the Central Committee in 1986. He remained an adviser to the central committee for some time afterward. Le Duc Tho died on Oct. 13, 1990, in Hanoi.

American troops began withdrawing from Vietnam in July 1969. Here, an American soldier boards a bus in Saigon, the South Vietnamese capital, that will take him to the airport for a flight back to the United States. The last U.S. ground forces left Vietnam on March 29, 1973.

CHAPTER FIVE

Final U.S. troop withdrawal and end of the war

The high cost paid by both sides during the 1972 fighting led to a new round of peace negotiations. The talks were conducted by Henry A. Kissinger, Nixon's chief foreign policy adviser, and Le Duc Tho (*lay duhk tow*) of North Vietnam. On Jan. 27, 1973, a cease-fire agreement was signed in Paris by the United States, South Vietnam, North Vietnam, and the Viet Cong. The pact provided for the withdrawal of all U.S. and allied forces from Vietnam and for the return of all prisoners—both within 60 days. It also permitted North Vietnam and the Viet Cong to leave their troops in the south. In addition, it called for internationally supervised elections that would let the South Vietnamese decide their political future.

On March 29, 1973, the last U.S. ground forces left Vietnam. But the peace talks soon broke down, and the war resumed. Congress, responding to voters who wished to see an end to the war, opposed further U.S. involvement. As a result, American troops did not return to the war. In mid-1973, Congress began to reduce military aid to South Vietnam.

Later that year, Congress passed the War Powers Resolution (popularly known as the War Powers Act). According to Section 4(a)(1) of the resolution, the president must inform Congress within 48 hours if U.S. forces are sent into a hostile area without a declaration of war. The forces may remain no longer than 60 days unless Congress approves the president's action or declares war. The president may extend this dead-

Henry Kissinger

Henry Alfred Kissinger (1923-) served as secretary of state of the United States from 1973 to 1977. He was appointed by President Richard M. Nixon and kept the post after Gerald R. Ford became president in 1974. Kissinger also served as assistant to the president for national security affairs from 1969 to 1975. He was the most influential foreign policy adviser of both presidents.

Between 1969 and 1973, Kissinger conducted secret negotiations with North Vietnamese diplomats to end the Vietnam War. The negotiations led to a cease-fire agreement signed in January 1973 by the United States, North Vietnam, South Vietnam, and the Viet Cong. Kissinger and Le Duc Tho, the chief North Vietnamese negotiator, won the 1973 Nobel Peace Prize for negotiating the cease-fire. But fighting continued until the war ended in 1975.

During Nixon's presidency, Kissinger enjoyed a high media profile and popularity. But the Nixon presidency lost credibility during the Watergate scandal, which began in 1972, and Kissinger's public support suffered. Ford retained him as secretary of state, but Kissinger grew controversial and subject to criticism. Republican conservatives objected to his policy of *détente* (easing of tensions) toward the Soviet Union, while Democrats disap-

U.S. Secretary of State Henry A. Kissinger (left) met with Egyptian President Anwar el-Sadat near Alexandria, Egypt, in 1975. Kissinger was the most influential U.S. foreign policy adviser in the 1970's.

proved of his secretive diplomacy. In 1983, President Ronald Reagan named Kissinger head of a federal commission to develop U.S. policy on Central America. From 2001 to 2005, Kissinger served as chancellor of the College of William and Mary.

Kissinger was born on May 27, 1923, in Furth, Germany. His family came to the United States in 1938 to escape Nazi persecution of Jews. Kissinger served in the U.S. Army during World War II. He became a U.S. citizen in 1943. Kissinger earned three degrees at Harvard University and taught courses there on international relations. His writings on foreign policy include *Nuclear Weapons and Foreign Policy* (1957). Kissinger has published three volumes of memoirs, *White House Years* (1979), *Years of Upheaval* (1982), and *Years of Renewal* (1999). *Diplomacy* (1994) deals with notable statesmen since the 1600's. Other books include *On China* (2011) and *World Order* (2014).

U.S. Secretary of State William Rogers (center), who served from 1969 to 1973 under President Richard M. Nixon, signed the Paris Peace Accords on Jan. 27, 1973. The accords called for the end of all hostilities, the withdrawal of U.S. and other foreign troops, and the return of prisoners of war.

line an additional 30 days.

The resolution was created because of actions taken by President Johnson and President Nixon during the Vietnam War. Both sent troops into battle even though Congress did not specifically approve such an action or declare war.

The resolution's 90-day limit has never been applied because no president who has ordered troops into combat areas since 1973 has referred to Section 4(a)(1) of the resolution. Instead, the presidents have referred to their constitutional authority as commander in chief.

Congress took its first major action under the resolution in 1983 after U.S. Marines in Lebanon were attacked. President Ronald Reagan

In March 1975, North Vietnam forced South Vietnamese troops to retreat from a region known as the Central Highlands. Thousands of civilians (shown above) who fled with the troops died in the gunfire or from starvation. This retreat became known as the Convoy of Tears.

Final U.S. troop withdrawal and end of the war

reported the situation. But he disagreed with Congress that the 90-day limit of the War Powers Resolution had been triggered because he did not mention Section 4(a)(1) in his report. Congress later passed a law allowing the troops to remain in Lebanon for 18 months.

In late 1974, North Vietnamese and Viet Cong troops won an easy victory when they attacked Phuoc (*fook*) Long, northeast of Saigon. In March 1975, the North Vietnamese forced South Vietnamese troops into a retreat from a region known as the Central Highlands. Thousands of

On April 30, 1975, Communist North Vietnamese troops in tanks and trucks rolled into Saigon, the South Vietnamese capital. South Vietnam's government formally surrendered, ending the Vietnam War. Saigon was renamed Ho Chi Minh City by the North Vietnam government in honor of its Communist leader Ho Chi Minh.

civilians—many of them families of the South Vietnamese soldiers—also fled and died in the gunfire or from starvation. This retreat became known as the Convoy of Tears. Although some South Vietnamese army units fought on, few soldiers or civilians rallied in support of the failing South Vietnamese government.

Early in April, President Gerald R. Ford asked Congress for $722 million in military aid for South Vietnam. But Congress, believing defeat was now inevitable, provided only $300 million in emergency aid. The

Final U.S. troop withdrawal and end of the war

Nguyen Van Thieu

Nguyen Van Thieu (1923-2001) became president of South Vietnam in 1967, during the Vietnam War. In April 1975—under heavy pressure from his non-Communist political opponents—Thieu resigned from office in an attempt to encourage cease-fire talks between the Communists and the South Vietnam government. But the Vietnam War ended about a week later with a Communist takeover of South Vietnam.

Thieu was South Vietnam's deputy prime minister and defense minister in 1965. From 1965 to 1967, he served as chief of state and chairman of the Directory, a 10-member executive committee in the military government that ruled South Vietnam.

Two developments triggered public frustrations into the strongest challenge ever to Thieu's presidency. One was the resignation on Aug. 9, 1974, of U.S. President Richard M. Nixon, a strong supporter of Thieu. Nixon's fall seemed to prove to many of Thieu's opponents that the Vietnamese president might also be vulnerable. The other was U.S. congressional cuts in military aid for South Vietnam. Instead of the requested $1.45 billion for the period from July 1, 1974, to June 30, 1975, Congress voted only $700 million. In the face of the cuts, the South Vietnamese Army had to reduce its use of planes, bombs, artillery shells, and other supplies. The resulting fears of military weakness sparked demands for new efforts to reach a political settlement with the

Communists rather than accept Thieu's insistence that a political deal would be suicidal.

The two main groups agitating against Thieu were a Roman Catholic-led "People's Movement Against Corruption, for National Salvation and Peace Restoration" and "The Forces for National Reconciliation" led by the An Quang faction of Buddhists.

Thieu moved gradually to meet the demonstrators' complaints of corruption. In October, he fired 377 army majors and colonels and three generals commanding regions of Vietnam. He also reshuffled his Cabinet. Among the ministers he dropped was Hoang Duc Nha, his cousin and top adviser on relations with Washington. But such moves failed to satisfy the opponents. The People's Movement anticorruption leader, Tran Huu Thanh, continued to call for Thieu's resignation, as did others. Thieu denied the corruption charges and told the nation that he would resign "if the entire people and army no longer have confidence in me."

The Viet Cong continued its full-scale war against the Saigon government. On October 8, it called for Thieu's overthrow, saying it would not negotiate with his regime under cease-fire agreement terms.

Thieu was born in Phan Rang on April 5, 1923. Born a Buddhist, he became a Roman Catholic in 1958. As a military officer, he led a major attack during the military revolt that overthrew President Ngo Dinh Diem of South Vietnam in 1963. After the Communists took control of South Vietnam in 1975, Thieu fled to London, in the United Kingdom. He later settled outside Boston, in the United States. He died in Boston on Sept. 29, 2001.

Two Vietnamese women visited South Vietnam's national military cemetery at Bien Hoa in 1975 to mourn their relatives who died in the Vietnam War. South Vietnamese military losses were about 224,000 killed and 1 million wounded. Countless numbers of South and North Vietnamese civilians also died in the conflict.

Final U.S. troop withdrawal and end of the war   109

The Vietnam War made refugees of as many as 10 million people in South Vietnam. After the fall of the capital Saigon, many South Vietnamese fled the country in small boats and ships seeking refuge from the invading Communist forces from North Vietnam. These refugees were widely referred to as "boat people."

money was mainly for the evacuation of Americans from Saigon, which was threatened by rapidly advancing enemy troops. Also that month—under heavy pressure from his non-Communist political opponents—Nguyen Van Thieu, the South Vietnamese president, resigned from office in an attempt to encourage cease-fire talks between the Communists and the South Vietnam government, but the war would end a week later. The war ended on April 30, 1975, when North Vietnamese troops entered Saigon and the South Vietnamese government formally surrendered to

In 1976, North and South Vietnam were united into a single nation, which was renamed the Socialist Republic of Vietnam. The new 500-member National Assembly for a united Vietnam held its first session (shown above) in July.

them. Saigon was then renamed Ho Chi Minh City.

After the Communists took control of South Vietnam, Thieu fled to London, in the United Kingdom. He later settled outside Boston, Massachusetts, in the United States.

More than 58,000 American military personnel died in the war. About 300,000 others were wounded. South Vietnamese military losses were about 224,000 killed and 1 million wounded. North Vietnamese and Viet Cong losses totaled about 1 million dead and 600,000 wounded. Countless numbers of civilians in North and South Vietnam also perished.

The U.S. bombing in the conflict was more than three times as great as the combined U.S.-British bombing of Germany in World War II. The

North Vietnam helped establish Communist governments in Cambodia and Laos in 1975. This image shows many Cambodian refugees fleeing the capital Phnom Penh after Cambodian Communists called Khmer Rouge took control of Cambodia.

American air strikes destroyed much of North Vietnam's industrial and transportation systems. But South Vietnam, where most of the fighting took place, suffered the most damage. The bombing and use of chemicals to clear forests scarred the landscape and may have permanently damaged much of South Vietnam's cropland and plant and animal life.

The war made refugees of as many as 10 million South Vietnamese. Many refugees left Vietnam in small boats, risking drowning and pirate attacks in the South China Sea. These refugees became known as *boat people*. They went to other countries in Southeast Asia, where they stayed in refugee camps until they could be relocated. Many later settled in the United States, Australia, and Canada, or joined earlier generations of exiles in Belgium and France. In the mid-1990's, the UN and countries that housed or helped pay for the camps closed nearly all of them. Most of the remaining refugees were sent back to Vietnam.

In 1976, North and South Vietnam were united into a single nation, which was renamed the Socialist Republic of Vietnam. North Vietnamese leaders then forced their own rigid political culture on people of the south. They imprisoned thousands who had held positions of responsibility in the South Vietnamese army or government. They also waged a campaign against independent businesses, run mainly by Vietnamese merchants of Chinese descent. As a result, over 1 million Vietnamese fled Vietnam between 1975 and the early 1990's, and the economy stagnated. But the harsh social divisions between Vietnamese rich and poor were ended, and literacy rates soared.

North Vietnam had helped establish Communist governments in Laos and Cambodia in 1975. During the late stages of the Vietnam War in the early 1970's, Cambodian Communists called Khmer Rouge (*kuh MEHR ROOZH*), or Red Khmers, were engaging in full-scale warfare against the country's non-Communist government. In April 1975, they took control of Cambodia. Cambodian President Lon Nol fled to the United States in 1975, shortly before the rebels took control of the government. The former king, Sihanouk, was allowed to return to Cambodia as head of state, but he had no real political power.

The anti-Vietnamese policies of the pro-Chinese Communist Khmer Rouge movement in Cambodia forced Vietnam into a lengthy and costly campaign in that country. China reacted to this evidence of Vietnam's growing influence in the region by briefly invading Vietnam in 1979.

In January 1979, Vietnamese troops and allied Cambodian Communists won control of most of Cambodia and overthrew the Khmer Rouge government. The victorious Cambodians renamed the country the People's Republic of Kampuchea. The Vietnamese supported the new government and gained much influence in the country. Strict control of the lives of the people continued under the new government.

The Khmer Rouge continued to fight the Vietnamese and their Cambodian allies. Non-Communist groups also joined in the fighting. In 1982, non-Communists and the Khmer Rouge formed a coalition. Sihanouk became head of the coalition. The fighting forced hundreds of thousands of Cambodians into refugee camps during the 1980's.

In the 1980's, the government took steps to reduce its control of the economy. These included allowing Cambodians to own their own small businesses and farms. In addition, Vietnam gradually withdrew troops from Cambodia. In September 1989, Vietnam said that it had completed the withdrawal. Also in 1989, Cambodia's government and opposition groups began negotiations to resolve the war. In October 1991, they signed a UN-sponsored peace treaty. Under the treaty, the United Nations supervised Cambodia in 1992 through a transition to democracy.

During the Vietnam War, the U.S. Central Intelligence Agency (CIA) recruited and trained a "secret army" in Laos to fight the Communists.

Vietnamese refugees arrive at an air station in the United States after being evacuated from Saigon, South Vietnam's capital, in 1975. The refugees, fleeing a Communist takeover of their country, would later be transported to the U.S. Marine Corps Base at Camp Pendleton, California.

This army was drawn mainly from the Hmong (*mawng*), also called *Meo* or *Miao*, a mountain people that have traditionally farmed for a living. Following the North Vietnamese victory in Vietnam in April 1975, thousands of Hmong and other Laotians fled Laos. Many Hmong who stayed were persecuted and imprisoned by the Communist-inspired Pathet Lao movement that gained control of Laos.

Laos had been fighting a civil war during the Vietnam War, resulting from factional disputes that started in the early 1950's. Laos gained

Vietnam Veterans Memorial

The Vietnam Veterans Memorial in Washington, D.C., honors the Americans who served in the Vietnam War. The memorial, which includes three separate parts, stands on the National Mall. It features two black granite walls that meet at an angle. The names of over 58,000 Americans, who died in the war or who remained classified as missing in action when the walls were built in 1982, are inscribed on the walls. The memorial also includes Frederick Hart's large, bronze Three Soldiers statue, which was added in 1984, and Glenna Goodacre's Vietnam Women's Memorial statue, which was added in 1993. In 2004, officials dedicated a plaque that honors service members who died after the war from injuries suffered in Vietnam.

The Vietnam Veterans Memorial honors Americans who served in the Vietnam War. The black granite walls shown here hold the names of soldiers who died in Vietnam or were classified as missing in action.

The Vietnam Veterans Memorial, in Washington, D.C., includes the Three Soldiers sculpture (left), which features three American servicemen. Each year, millions of people visit the memorial and lay flowers at its base.

In 1979, the Vietnam Veterans Memorial Fund, Inc. (VVMF) was formed to establish the memorial. The VVMF raised over $8 million through private contributions. It held a national competition to select a design. Maya Ying Lin, then a student at Yale University, designed the two walls. Each wall is about 245 feet (75 meters) long, and the two meet at an angle of about 125 degrees. A walkway in front of the walls slants down from the ends of the walls to the meeting point. At the top of the slant, the walls extend only a few inches above the walkway. At the bottom of the slant, where the walls meet, the walls extend about 10 feet (3 meters) above the walkway. Visitors to the memorial can use directories to find the names of specific servicemen and servicewomen.

The flag-draped coffins bearing the remains of nine American servicemen killed during the Vietnam War are returned to the United States and unloaded from a U.S. Air Force transport plane.

complete independence from France in 1953. Meanwhile, the Free Laos movement had split into several factions. In northeastern Laos, Souphanouvong (*soo fahn oh vawng*), the leader of one of the factions, set up the Pathet Lao movement.

The Geneva Accords of 1954 left the two northeastern provinces of Laos under Pathet Lao control. The rest of the country was ruled by the Royal Lao Government (RLG) with Souvanna Phouma (*soo VAH nah FOO mah*) as prime minister. In 1957, Souvanna Phouma and Souphanouvong formed a coalition government and reunited the country under the RLG administration. The coalition collapsed, however, and in 1959, Laos plunged into civil war. A second coalition government was agreed upon in 1962. But that government also failed, and in 1963, government and Pathet Lao forces resumed fighting each other.

Laos tried to remain neutral during the Vietnam War but was increasingly drawn into the conflict in the early 1960's partly due to CIA secret recruitment of Hmong people. Also, from the mid-1960's until 1973, U.S. warplanes heavily bombed sections of Laos, particularly the Ho Chi Minh Trail in the eastern part of the country. With North Vietnam helping establish a Communist regime, the Pathet Lao finally gained power and abolished the monarchy in December 1975.

The Vietnam War also had far-reaching effects in the United States, which spent about $200 billion on the war. Many experts believe that this high cost of the war damaged the U.S. economy for years after the war's conclusion.

Vietnam veterans

The Vietnam War was the first foreign war in which U.S. combat forces failed to achieve their goals. This failure hurt the pride of many Americans and left bitter and painful memories. The Americans most immediately affected included the approximately 2,600,000 men and women who had served in the war, as well as their families. Most Vietnam veterans adjusted smoothly to civilian life. But others, particularly those with psychological problems associated with combat stress, encountered difficulties in making the adjustment to postwar American society. These veterans suffered from high rates of divorce, drug abuse, unemployment, and homelessness.

After World War I (1914-1918) and World War II (1939-1945), the country viewed its soldiers as heroes. Americans who opposed the U.S. role in

Maya Lin

Maya Lin (1959-   ) is an American artist known for designing such architectural projects as monuments and parks. She became famous for her design for the Vietnam Veterans Memorial (1982), which stands in Washington, D.C. The memorial honors the Americans who served in the Vietnam War (1957-1975). Lin submitted her winning design in a national competition while she was a 21-year-old senior at Yale University. Lin's architectural work features abstract designs that harmonize with the surrounding landscape. Natural features of the earth, such as waves and hills, serve as inspiration for many of her sculptures.

Lin's other important projects include the Civil Rights Memorial (1989) in Montgomery, Alabama; Hope Plaza (2010) at Washington University in St. Louis; and a new building (2009) for the Museum of Chinese in America in New York City. Lin's outdoor installations include the *Wave Field* (1995) at the University of Michigan in Ann Arbor and the *Storm King Wavefield* (2009) in upstate New York. Both consist of rows of small rolling hills shaped like ocean waves. *A Fold in the Field* (2013) is an even larger earthwork north of Auckland, New Zealand, that continues the wave theme. The installation depicts five folds in the Earth set on a flat plain. Beginning in 2006, Lin has served as an artist and architect for the Confluence Project, a series of six outdoor works being built

The Vietnam Veterans Memorial includes the black granite memorial walls that Maya Lin (left) designed, the Three Soldiers statue (both are shown on pages 116 and 117), as well as the Vietnam Women's Memorial sculpture (right), which honors the American women who served in the military during the Vietnam War.

at historical spots along the Columbia River Basin in Oregon and Washington. In 2015, Lin was chosen to lead the redesign of the library at Smith College in Northampton, Massachusetts. Lin has also exhibited sculptures and furniture designs.

Maya Ying Lin was born on Oct. 5, 1959, in Athens, Ohio. Her parents had emigrated from China to the United States in 1949. Lin received a Bachelor of Arts degree in 1981, a Master of Architecture degree in 1986, and an honorary Doctor of Fine Arts degree in 1987, all from Yale University. She was the subject of *Maya Lin: A Strong Clear Vision* (1994), which won the Academy Award as best documentary motion picture of 1994. In 2016, she was awarded the United States' Presidential Medal of Freedom.

Vietnam had embraced those veterans who joined the antiwar movement upon their return from the battlefield, but some criticized or shunned those veterans who felt the war was justified. Many Americans who supported the war came to regard Vietnam veterans as symbols of America's defeat. Some leading hawks opposed expanding benefits to Vietnam veterans to match those given to veterans of earlier wars. These reactions shocked the veterans. Many of them felt that the nation neither recognized nor appreciated their sacrifices.

While this was happening, the American Legion, the largest veterans' organization in the United States, worked to increase veterans' benefits under the GI Bill to meet rising educational costs. The Legion also promoted job opportunities for returning veterans during and after the Vietnam War. After the war, the United States Congress and the public became more willing to challenge the president on military and foreign policy. The war also became a standard of comparison in situations that might involve U.S. troops abroad.

In the early 1990's, Democratic Senator John Kerry of Massachusetts, who had been a vocal opponent of the war after returning from naval service in Vietnam in 1970, chaired a special Senate committee investigating the fate of American soldiers declared missing in action during the Vietnam War. Some people believed that many soldiers were still being held captive in prison camps in Southeast Asia, but the committee found no evidence that such camps existed.

Kerry and Republican Senator John McCain of Arizona were then successful in bringing about the lifting of U.S. trade sanctions against Vietnam and the renewal of diplomatic relations.

Kerry enlisted in the U.S. Navy in 1966 and served until 1970. During that time, he spent about five months in combat in the Vietnam War. He was wounded in battle and received three Purple Heart citations and

U.S. Senator J. William Fulbright, Chairman of the Senate Foreign Relations Committee, listened to testimony in 1971 from Vietnam War veteran John Kerry (center), who became a leader of the antiwar group Vietnam Veterans Against the War.

Silver Star and Bronze Star medals. After completing his tour of duty in the Navy, Kerry helped found Vietnam Veterans of America, and he became a leader and spokesperson for the antiwar group Vietnam Veterans Against the War. Kerry was the Democratic presidential nominee in 2004. He lost to his Republican opponent, President George W. Bush. Kerry later served as U.S. secretary of state from 2013 to 2017.

McCain served as a fighter pilot during the Vietnam War. He entered the Navy after graduating from the United States Naval Academy in 1958. In 1967, during the Vietnam War, his plane was shot down over

Final U.S. troop withdrawal and end of the war   123

Vietnam, and he was held captive as a prisoner of war for over five years, until 1973. McCain received a Purple Heart medal for wounds he suffered during combat. He also received the Bronze Star and Silver Star medals for his service and bravery. McCain was the Republican nominee for president of the United States in the 2008 election.

Political refugees; lessons of war

Millions of Southeast Asians have come to the United States since the mid-1970's. Most of them fled their homelands because of the Vietnam War. The first wave to arrive were Vietnamese political refugees who

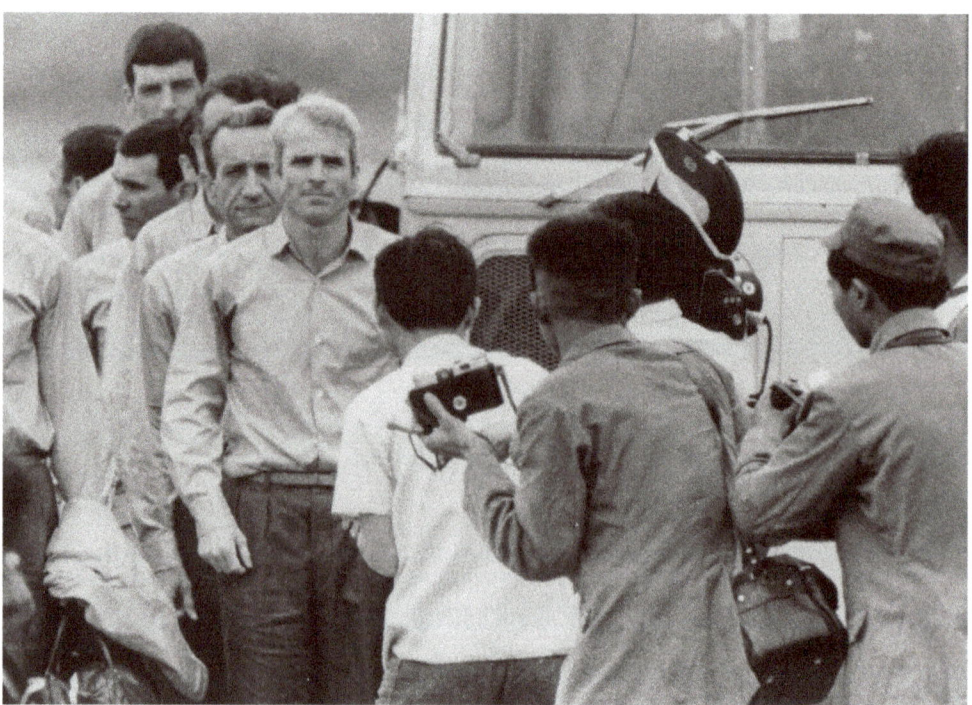

John McCain (center, with light hair) was among a group of American servicemen released from a prisoner of war camp in Vietnam in 1973. McCain was a fighter pilot during the Vietnam War before his plane was shot down in 1967. He was captured by the North Vietnamese and held for over five years.

had worked for the U.S. government or U.S. companies. For the most part, they were educated, skilled workers. Most of the second wave were rural people from Cambodia and Laos, who had less education and fewer job skills.

About three-fourths of the Southeast Asian immigrants settled in 10 states: California, Florida, Massachusetts, Minnesota, New York, Pennsylvania, Texas, Virginia, Washington, and Wisconsin. The initial response in most communities where the refugees settled was sympathetic. But in some cases, conflicts arose with local residents when the newcomers began to move into the labor force. Many Vietnamese refugees, for example, found jobs in the shrimp fishing industry in Mississippi, Texas, and other Gulf Coast States. Local fishing crews accused the Southeast Asians of setting too many traps, fishing in areas claimed by American crews, and other offenses. Fighting often broke out, and vandals on both sides damaged their rivals' boats and fishing nets.

Today, Americans still disagree on the main issues and lessons of the war. Some believe U.S. participation was necessary and just. Many of these people say the war was lost because the United States did not use its full military power and because opposition at home weakened the war effort. Others point to the failure of the South Vietnamese government to develop popular support and to its overreliance on the United States. Still others view U.S. involvement in Vietnam as immoral and unwise. Some of them feel American leaders made the war a test of the nation's power and leadership. Some view the conflict as a civil war that had no importance to U.S. security. Since Vietnam, many Americans have argued that the nation should stay out of wars that do not directly threaten its safety or vital interests.

INDEX

Abrams, Creighton, 41
Agent Orange, 66-68
Agnew, Spiro T., 83
Air Force, U.S., 28, 50, 51, 53
airplanes, 41, 44-45, 50-51, 53
Ali, Muhammad, 63
American Legion, 122
An Duong, 14
Army, U.S., 34, 40, 41, 46, 90; My Lai massacre, 60-61; weapons, 50
Associated State of Vietnam, 22-23
Associated States of Indochina, 9-11
August Revolution, 19
Australia, 6, 41, 46-49

Bacon, Robert, 40
Bayh, Birch Evans, Jr., 54, 70
Berrigan, Daniel and Philip, 87-91
boat people, 110, 113
Brown, Edmund G. (Pat), 81
Buddhists, 36, 37, 107
Bush, George W., 123

C. Turner Joy, USS, 38
Calley, William L., 60-64
Cambodia, 5, 6, 46, 54, 59, 125; Communist control, 112-114; French control, 9-11, 17-18; U.S. military campaign, 59-60, 71, 75, 84, 87
cancer, 66-68
Catonsville Nine, 87-90
Centers for Disease Control, 66
Central Intelligence Agency (CIA), 114-115, 119
China, 18, 81, 114; civil war, 9, 14; occupation of Vietnam, 14-17; support for Communists, 6, 9, 41, 46, 71, 84
Civil War, U.S., 62
Clifford, Clark, 58-59
Cold War, 5
Communism, 5-6, 10, 78; Ho Chi Minh and, 9, 10; in Indochina, 5-6, 14, 19-20; Le Luc Tho and, 94-97; Vo Nguyen Gap and, 24-25. *See also* North Vietnam; Viet Cong
Congress, U.S., 60, 62-63, 77; opposition to war, 54-57; presidential powers and, 87, 99-105; Tonkin Gulf Resolution, 38-39; veterans and, 122
conscientious objectors, 62-63
Convoy of Tears, 103-105
Cooper, John, 54

Da Nang, 17, 36
Defense, Department of, 68, 69
Democratic Party, 77, 83, 122, 123
Democratic Republic of Vietnam (DRV), 20, 24. *See also* North Vietnam
Detroit, 79-80
Diem, Ngo Dinh, 27, 29-37, 49, 74, 107
Dien Bien Phu, Battle of, 8, 12-13, 20-22
dioxins, 66
Dong, Pham Van, 26, 41
doves, 49-54, 78
draft, 46, 62-63, 87, 90

Eisenhower, Dwight D., 6, 27, 71, 74, 77
Ellsberg, Daniel, 69-71

First Amendment, 71
flame throwers, 66
Fonda, Jane, 91-94
Ford, Gerald R., 100, 105
France, 5, 6, 49, 118; First Indochina War, 8-13, 20-24; rule over Indochina, 17-19
Fulbright, J. William, 54, 123

Geneva Accords, 22-27, 96, 118
Going After Cacciato (O'Brien), 34, 35
Goldwater, Barry M., 78
Goodacre, Glenna, 116
guerrillas, 30, 46, 96
Gulf of Tonkin Resolution, 37-39, 60

Haiphong, 9
Hanoi, 9, 11, 84, 92
Hart, Frederick, 116
hawks, 49-54, 78, 122
helicopters, 41, 46, 52
Hmong, 115, 119
Ho Chi Minh, 9-11, 14, 19-20, 23-27, 94-96

Ho Chi Minh Trail, 29, 119
Humphrey, Hubert H., 54, 78, 83

Indochina, 5-6; early, 15; First War, 8-13, 20-24; French, 17-19
Institute of Medicine, 66-68

Japan, 18-19
Jeannette Rankin Brigade, 55-57
Johnson, Lyndon B., 6, 43, 49, 71, 102; policies, 37-39, 49-54, 58-59, 76-81

Kampuchea, 114
Kennedy, John F., 6, 29-36, 71, 75, 77, 78, 81
Kennedy, Robert F., 54, 78-79
Kent State shooting, 60, 61, 84
Kerner, Otto, 80
Kerry, John, 60, 122-123
Khmer Rouge, 113, 114
Kissinger, Henry A., 86, 87, 94, 95, 97, 99-101
Kosygin, Aleksei, 79

Laos, 5-7, 36, 46, 66, 125; Communist victory, 113-119; French control, 11, 12, 17-18
Le Duc Tho, 94-97, 100
Le dynasty, 16-17
Lin, Maya Ying, 117, 120-121
Lodge, Henry Cabot, Jr., 36
Long Tan, Battle of, 46-49

Mac dynasty, 16-17
Maddox, USS, 37-39
Manila, Philippines, 79, 80
Marines, U.S., 39, 46, 102
Marshall Plan, 22
Matak, Prince Sisowath Sirik, 59-60
McAlister, Elizabeth, 91
McCain, John, 122-124
McCarthy, Eugene, 54, 55, 78-79
McGovern, George S., 84
McNamara, Robert, 71, 75
Miller, William E., 78
Muskie, Edmund S., 83
My Lai massacre, 60-64, 75

napalm, 65-66

National Liberation Front (NLF), 30, 81
Navy, U.S., 50, 51, 60, 122-124
New Jersey, USS, 50, 51
New York Times, The, 68-69
New Zealand, 6, 41
Ngo Quyen, 14, 15
Nguyen dynasty, 17
Nhu, Ngo Dinh, 36
Nixon, Richard, 97; policies, 59-60, 74-75, 81-87, 102; Watergate and resignation, 71, 81, 100, 106
Nixon Doctrine, 83
Nobel Peace Prize, 90, 94
Nol, Lon, 59-60, 114
Norodom Palace, 16
North Vietnam, 5-6, 11, 27, 49-50, 59, 92; cease-fire with, 86, 97, 99; destruction in, 112-113; leaders, 10, 24-25, 94-97; origin, 20, 23, 26; strategy, 46; U.S. military campaign, 29, 36-39, 41, 46, 50, 58, 71-78, 80-81; victories by, 104-113
Nui Dat, 47-48

O'Brien, Tim, 34-35

Paris, 59, 81, 83; Peace Accords, 72-73, 86, 97, 99, 102
Pathet Lao, 115-119
Pentagon Papers, 68-71
Philippines, 6, 41, 79, 80
Plumbers, 71

Rankin, Jeannette, 54-57
Reagan, Ronald, 83, 101-103
refugees, 103, 110, 113-115, 124-125
Republican Party, 77, 81-83, 122, 124
riots, 60, 79-80, 94
Rockefeller, Nelson, 83
Rogers, William, 102
Roman Catholicism, 36, 91, 107
Rusk, Dean, 43
Russo, Anthony J., Jr., 71

Sadat, Anwar el-, 101
Saigon, 6, 47, 98, 104-105, 107, 110-112, 115
"search and destroy" missions, 40, 42

Shriver, Sargent, 84
Sihanouk, Norodom, 59-60, 114
Smith, Harry, 47-49
Souphanouvong, 118-119
South Korea, 6, 41
South Vietnam, 5-6, 10, 78, 96-97; Agent Orange in, 66-68; Australian troops in, 46-48; casualties, 112; fall of Diem, 28-37; invasion by North, 74; My Lai massacre, 60-64; origin, 27, 96; peace talks and U.S. withdrawal, 81, 83, 99, 104-105; refugees from, 110, 113-115, 124-125; surrender to North, 110-112; Thieu regime, 49, 106-107, 110; U.S. troops in, 39, 41, 46, 78, 83-84; U.S. withdrawal, 86; Vietnamization policy, 57-59, 69. *See also* Viet Cong
Souvanna Phouma, 118-119
Soviet Union, 23, 79, 81, 85, 100; support for Communists, 6, 9, 41, 46, 84
Supreme Court, U.S., 63, 69-71

Tay Son Rebellion, 17
Taylor, Maxwell D., 71, 75
Tet Offensive, 57-58
Thailand, 6, 41
Thieu, Nguyen Van, 49, 106-107, 110-112
Things They Carried, The (O'Brien), 34, 35
Three Soldiers sculpture, 116, 117, 121
Tourane, 36
Trinh lords, 17
Truman, Harry S., 5-6, 14, 71
Truman Doctrine, 5-6

"Uncounted Enemy, The" (TV program), 42
United Nations (UN), 72-73, 113, 114
United States, 5-7; aid to France, 9-11, 14; casualties, 112; opposition to Communism, 19-27. *See also* Vietnam War

Van Lang, 14

veterans, 119-124; health problems, 66-68; memorial, 116-117, 120-121
Viet Cong, 30-33, 37, 39, 50, 65, 96-97, 107; at war's end, 99, 100, 104; deaths, 112; forces and tactics, 41-46, 83; in Long Tan battle, 47-49; in Tet Offensive, 57, 58; origin, 29, 30
Vietminh, 9-14, 18-21, 29, 30
Vietnam, 5; declaration of independence, 19-20; French attempt to reclaim, 8-14, 21-22; history through 1956, 14-27; refugees from, 110, 113-115, 124-125; reunification, 110-113. *See also* North Vietnam; South Vietnam
Vietnam Veterans Against the War, 60, 93, 123
Vietnam Veterans Memorial, 116-117, 120-121
Vietnam War, 5-7; background, 9-27; casualties, 6, 112; Diem, fall of, 29-36; dissent and protest in U.S., 7, 49-56, 60, 87-94; Johnson policies, 37-39, 49, 58-59, 76-81; limits on presidential power and, 99-104; Nixon policies, 59-60, 74-75, 81-87, 102; *Pentagon Papers* and, 68-71; strategies and weapons, 40-45, 50-53, 65-66; Tet Offensive and, 57-58; troop withdrawal by U.S., 98-110; veterans, problems of, 60-68, 119-124; victory by Communist forces, 104-119
Vietnamization policy, 59, 75, 84
Vo Nguyen Giap, 24-25

War Powers Resolution, 87, 99-104
Washington Post, The, 69
Watergate scandal, 71, 81, 100
Westmoreland, William C., 41-43, 58
Weyland, Frederick, 41
World War I, 62, 119-122
World War II, 9, 18-21, 90, 96, 112, 119-122

Zhou Enlai, 26

Index   127

FIND OUT MORE!

Blohm, Craig E. *Cause and Effect: The Vietnam War.* ReferencePoint, 2018.

National Archives: Vietnam War. https://www.archives.gov/research/vietnam-war

Smithsonian Institution. *The Vietnam War: The Definitive Illustrated History.* Dorling Kindersley, 2017.

Ward, Geoffrey C. and Burns, Ken. *The Vietnam War: An Intimate History.* Knopf, 2017.

ACKNOWLEDGMENTS

Cover:	National Archives; © Everett Historical/Shutterstock; © Larry Burrows, Time Magazine/The LIFE Picture Collection/Getty Images; U.S. Army; © Jacques Pavlovsky, Getty Images	40	© Larry Burrows, Time Magazine/The LIFE Picture Collection/Getty Images	92-93	© Jaguar PS/Shutterstock; © ADN-Bildarchiv/ullstein bild/Getty Images
		42-43	U.S. Army; National Archives	95	The White House Photo Office Collection
		44-45	U.S. Air Force	98	© AP Photo
		47	WORLD BOOK map	100-101	Library of Congress
4	National Archives	48	Mattinbgn (licensed under CC BY 3.0)	102-103	National Archives; © Bettmann/Getty Images
7	U.S. Army/National Archives	51	U.S. Navy; U.S. Air Force		
8	© Keystone/Getty Images	52-53	U.S. Air Force; Department of Defense; U.S. Air Force	104-105	© Jacques Pavlovsky, Getty Images
10-11	Public Domain; © Sovfoto/UIG/Getty Images			106	© Corbis/Getty Images
		55	© Bettmann/Getty Images	108-109	© Francoise Demulder, AFP/Getty Images
12-13	© Corbis/Getty Images; © Collection Jean-Claude Labbe/Gamma-Rapho/Getty Images	56	Library of Congress; © Glasshouse Images/Alamy Images	110-111	U.S. Navy; © Sovfoto/UIG/Getty Images
				112	© AFP/Getty Images
15	WORLD BOOK map	58	WORLD BOOK map	115	National Archives
16	Public Domain	61	© Bettmann/Getty Images	116-117	© Brandon Bourdages, Shutterstock; © Hang Dinh, Shutterstock
19	WORLD BOOK map				
20-21	© Collection Jean-Claude LABBE/Gamma-Rapho/Getty Images	63	Library of Congress		
		64-65	© Bettmann/Getty Images; National Archives	118	© Bettmann/Getty Images
22-23	© Frank Scherschel, The LIFE Picture Collection/Getty Images			120-121	Oregon State University (licensed under CC BY-SA 2.0); © Travel View/Shutterstock
		67	© Everett Historical/Shutterstock		
25	© SeM/UIG/Getty Images	68	Department of Defense		
26	© Keystone-France/Gamma-Keystone/Getty Images	70	Library of Congress	123	© Bettmann/Getty Images
		72-73	© Henri Bureau, Getty Images		
28	© Everett Historical/Shutterstock	74-75	National Archives; John F. Kennedy Presidential Library and Museum	124	National Archives
30-31	U.S. Army				
32-33	© Three Lions/Hulton Archive/Getty Images	76	The White House		
		79	U.S. Information Agency		
34	Greg Helgeson, Fall for the Book	80	National Archives		
		82	The White House		
37	© Bettmann/Getty Images	85-86	National Archives		
		89-90	© Bettmann/Getty Images		
38-39	U.S. Navy				

www.ingramcontent.com/pod-product-compliance
Lightning Source LLC
Chambersburg PA
CBHW060948170426
43201CB00023B/2417